Praise for *Make*

'*Make Your Own Map* is an absolute gift – to yourself, to your best friends, to your mentees. It is the guide I've being searching for when trying to help others define their journey and their destination. Kathryn Bishop's application of corporate strategy at an individual level not only facilitates an effective, adaptable and practicable "strategy for you", it also details the real-world implementation and experimentation necessary to realise your strategic purpose. Applicable to all, but mindful of the particular work–home challenges women may face during the evolution of their career, this is a guide to read with relish – and revisit!'
DR KATHERINE LEIVESLEY, MANAGING COUNSEL, KINGFISHER PLC

'Wonderfully practical and easy to read – I wish I had had this book when I made a fairly radical transition from one career into another, and I'm glad to have it now. The book is elegantly structured and the different stages introduced with great clarity, alongside carefully curated case studies to aid understanding. Kathryn Bishop's many years' experience gives her a calm and authoritative voice to guide the reader through the many and various models and ideas that help define purpose and success and lead towards real-world solutions. This is a book for busy women who crave focus and strategic insight in order to plan ahead – definitely one for the knapsack as you navigate your way through your (working) life.' PHYLLIDA HANCOCK, SENIOR PROGRAMME DIRECTOR, OLIVIER MYTHODRAMA, AND FREELANCE FACILITATOR AND COACH

'Whether you are lost, having to re-route because of an obstacle or just checking you are on the right path to reach your destination, everyone needs a map. This book is packed with clear guidance, useful exercises and thought-provoking case studies which are particularly designed for women managing their busy lives and juggling the multiple demands on their time.' JAN CAMERON, CIVIL SERVICE COMMISSIONER

'Not only has the content in this book been life changing for me, but I have led multiple clients through the exercises that Kathryn Bishop teaches in this book and each one has found them immensely helpful. For any person who finds themselves at a bit of a crossroads professionally, the context, teachings and case studies in this text have the ability to help you get unstuck and move from the passenger side to the driver's seat of your life. This is a must read for any woman looking to intentionally uplevel their career.' AMY YOUNG, FOUNDER AND CEO, REDEFINE POSSIBILITY, HEAD OF COACHING AND ENTERPRISE, SWAYWORKPLACE, CERTIFIED CAREER COACH AND FORMER HEAD OF GLOBAL PARTNERSHIPS, GOOGLE

'What a fantastic guide to plotting and navigating your career. Straightforward, easy to follow, and just the right mix of the strategic and the tactical. As our working lives get longer and many of us will have more than one career, this guide will help (any/every) woman plot her course. Having a career map will ensure that no matter the detour, one will always know that a temporary setback is not a "dead-end", and be able to navigate a way through and continue on the path to one's goals. That's a very powerful thing to be able to do. The examples of other women's journeys in the book are inspirational and make it real.' SARAH LAESSIG, PORTFOLIO NON-EXECUTIVE DIRECTOR

'A gamechanger! Practical, easy-to-follow, and 100% customizable to where I was in my life. This book will help any woman navigate the next steps in her career with clarity and focus. Kathryn Bishop understands the many roles that women juggle and why they need a book just for them. Her advice is based on years of research and practical experience coaching women on their careers. You can apply corporate strategy techniques to your life and ambitions, and this book shows you how.' ROBYN TINGLEY, CEO, GLASSSKY INC

'Create your own map is a companion style of book for women wanting to chart their career path. I can imagine in years to come hundreds of women with tatty worn copies in handbags everywhere, like a trusted friend, as the book is used repeatedly to refresh, remind and re-discover fantastic tools that helped them map their personal success story. It has helped me and I have relished reading it.' HAYLEY MONKS, DIRECTOR, THINK INSPIRE & CREATE LTD

'This book is simply refreshing with practical frameworks and models to assist you to navigate the different phases in your career. This process will ensure you come to a resolution about what success looks like for you and the steps that you need to take to get there. I found the book provided examples so that you don't feel alone in this balancing act of life. This book will certainly be a "go to" for me and having Kathryn explaining the process is like listening to your best friend.' DERINDA BROWN, DIRECTOR, MASTERCARD, ASIA PACIFIC

'Kathryn Bishop is a tour de force and learning from her and her experience is a privilege. She brings real-life perspectives to her teaching and I have found her to be relevant, balanced and empathetic to all points of view while helping to shape the individual story and actions. Her book carries the same trademark. Teacher, mentor, friend, colleague and coach – all wrapped into one for the best advice and practical strategies for YOU!' JHUMAR JOHNSON, DIRECTOR, VICE CHANCELLOR'S OFFICE, THE OPEN UNIVERSITY

Make Your Own Map

Career Success Strategy for Women

Kathryn Bishop

Kogan Page
INSPIRE

Publisher's note
Every possible effort has been made to ensure that the information contained in this book is accurate at the time of going to press, and the publishers and author cannot accept responsibility for any errors or omissions, however caused. No responsibility for loss or damage occasioned to any person acting, or refraining from action, as a result of the material in this publication can be accepted by the editor, the publisher or the author.

First published in Great Britain and the United States in 2021 by Kogan Page Limited

2nd Floor, 45 Gee Street	122 W 27th St, 10th Floor	4737/23 Ansari Road
London	New York, NY 10001	Daryaganj
EC1V 3RS	USA	New Delhi 110002
United Kingdom		India

www.koganpage.com

Kogan Page books are printed on paper from sustainable forests.

ISBNs

Hardback	978 1 78966 838 4
Paperback	978 1 78966 836 0
Ebook	978 1 78966 837 7

British Library Cataloguing-in-Publication Data

A CIP record for this book is available from the British Library.

Library of Congress Cataloging-in-Publication Data

Names: Bishop, Kathryn, 1958- author.
Title: Make your own map : career success strategy for women / Kathryn Bishop.
Description: London, United Kingdom ; New York, NY : Kogan Page, 2021. |
    Includes bibliographical references and index.
Identifiers: LCCN 2020050873 (print) | LCCN 2020050874 (ebook) | ISBN
    9781789668360 (paperback) | ISBN 9781789668384 (hardback) | ISBN
    9781789668377 (ebook)
Subjects: LCSH: Women–Vocational guidance. | Businesswomen. | Success in business.
Classification: LCC HD6058 .B66 2021 (print) | LCC HD6058 (ebook) | DDC 650.1082–dc23
LC record available at https://lccn.loc.gov/2020050873
LC ebook record available at https://lccn.loc.gov/2020050874

Typeset by Integra Software Services, Pondicherry
Print production managed by Jellyfish
Printed and bound by 4edge Ltd, UK

*For all the women I have worked with in organizations,
in lecture theatres and in coaching sessions, with the hope that
this book will be useful to them.
And for my mother, a woman who worked throughout her life
and supported me through mine.*

Contents

List of figures

About the author

Kathryn Bishop is an Associate Fellow at the Saïd Business School, University of Oxford, where she has taught strategy development to organizations and individuals for over 20 years. She is the Programme Director for Oxford University's leadership programme for women, Women Transforming Leadership, and has worked with women from all over the world as they make their career and development plans. In her teaching and in this book, Kathryn draws on 35 years of experience in working with organizations undergoing major change, in both the public and the private sectors – and with individuals leading those changes. Her background includes IT and HR and she has worked as a line director and manager, a project manager, a consultant and a non-executive director in both the private and public sectors.

Foreword

We know from our research in Oxford, examining the factors that shape women's leadership journeys and transitions, that women's working lives take many different directions. They are often both propelled and constrained by organizational and cultural changes. This gives women a particular navigation challenge as they seek to carve out meaningful roles in increasingly uncertain contexts. The ideas and exercises offered in this book will really help in dealing with this.

Over the last eight years, Kathryn has developed the ideas in this book and taught them on our programmes at Oxford, both residential and online, working with male and female leaders from all over the world. She has built up a remarkable evidence base of what helps leaders to have impact and deal with transitions in their roles. I have had the privilege of working with her, and I have seen that women who use these ideas and do the exercises find them transformational, helping them to think differently about their working life so far and their future plans.

You have the same opportunity – reflecting and rethinking using a set of well-researched and tailored frameworks. The book will help you whether you want to make a change in the direction of your working life, or simply some smaller changes in how you manage your current role. What is remarkable about the book is the range of different models and frameworks offered for you to reflect on what you would like to do or to change. There will definitely be one that helps you to see your route ahead more clearly.

This book will guide you through the process with explanations and examples, as well as Kathryn's wise and friendly advice.

Professor Sue Dopson
Rhodes Trust Professor of Organisational Behaviour,
Fellow of Green Templeton College, and Deputy Dean of
Saïd Business School at the University of Oxford

Preface: why this book is for you

Do you remember when you were a child what you wanted to be when you grew up? Maybe an astronaut or a ballerina, a chef or a doctor? Although you might have imagined what it would be like to *be* that person, you probably didn't know what it would be like to *do* that particular job, because you were too young. And as for how to get such a job, you may have thought that simply having the ambition was more than half the battle. But as you grew up, reality may have changed your plans, as it does for most of us. You may have had to change direction more than once. And maybe now you find yourself in a very different kind of role, but still with some unrealized ambitions, some unfulfilled longings. There's still somewhere you want to get to – whether or not you know exactly where that is.

This is a book about that journey, written for women who want to find a better way of working. Women who are looking for a role and context which suits them and in which they can contribute or make a difference. It's a book about turning some dreams into a workable reality. The book will help you to make your own map for a journey to a more fulfilled working life. It will help you to navigate through the turbulence of the working world and the demands of your private life. This is never simple; the road ahead isn't straight, and there aren't many shortcuts. And there are often strong winds that might blow you well and truly off the course that you planned.

Why this book is particularly for women

Everyone's working life is affected by their context – what's possible in terms of employment opportunities where they live, for example. Everyone has to find a new route when there is an economic crisis that bankrupts their employer. But women's working lives seem particularly affected by all sorts of external factors which can distort their plans. Over the last decade, I have worked with women from all over the world in different industries, doing a whole range of different jobs, as they wrestle with the challenge of working effectively at each stage of their life. Some of them were colleagues, some participants on executive education programmes, while others were friends or relatives. They've told me their stories at weddings, in cafes or on holidays. Many talked about the constraints they face from their responsibilities outside work. Some women knew that they wanted to make a change but were not sure when, where or how to make that change. Some were very clear about what they wanted to do, but many were not. Almost all these women knew what didn't work for them, but couldn't always define why. And they found it hard to see what kind of work would be better for them at that stage in their lives. They agreed to have their stories included in this book, in the hope that they might help you.

Here's an introduction to two of them, each of whom needed to find a new strategy for their working lives when their context changed suddenly.

CASE STUDY   A merger changes everything

Julie always said she didn't have any difficulty getting up in the morning because she loved her job. After eight years in the company, a national distribution business, she had been promoted to the perfect role: senior marketing manager. She knew the business well and particularly liked her colleagues in the sales teams who appreciated her support on large commercial bids. Her commute was easy and she could work from home at least once a week if she needed to. Finally – the right job!

And then one morning, just before Christmas, her employers announced that they were merging with another larger organization. Her heart sank. As usual, that announcement was followed by some major restructuring. The new merged business only needed one senior marketing manager, so Julie and her equivalent in the larger organization were told they could both apply for the job. But Julie wasn't sure that she wanted to do that. The new post would be in a different location, and she suspected that it would mostly involve a stream of merger-related activities, at least in the short term. And, of course, even if she applied, she might not get the job. What would happen then? Her salary was vital to her family; if she had to look for another role elsewhere, she might not find one quickly. She might have to take a salary cut, or even relocate, which could be a problem for her children at that stage in their education. Should she apply for the job or start looking for a new role elsewhere? Or both? Or was this the trigger for a change of direction? And if so, what? There were so many questions, and she didn't quite know where to find the answers.

CASE STUDY   Relocating requires some career choices

Lucy is a really good physiotherapist, as I discovered when I injured my shoulder. She has all her UK professional qualifications and a warm style of dealing with people in pain. In her late twenties she got married, and, within a year, her husband was posted to British Columbia in Canada. There, she found that she could neither practise nor apply for physiotherapy posts without a time-consuming registration process, because her UK qualifications weren't formally recognized. But she had to find some work, so she took a temporary job as an administrator in a local business. We emailed back and forth and she told me that, although the move to Canada was fun, it had definitely disrupted her career plans. 'I love being a physio, and I thought I could do it for ever – even if I want to take time out to have children, or to help my parents, who aren't getting any younger. So what do I do now? Do I go through the requalification process, even though it might be wasted effort if my husband is posted somewhere else? Is there something else I can do? Something similar which doesn't require me to requalify every time we have to relocate? What are my choices – and how shall I choose?'

Both Lucy and Julie had a plan for their working lives, until their circumstances changed. As a result, they needed to make a new map to navigate through some very different contexts, which brought a range of new options. And that's what this book is for: to help women like them – and like you – to do just that.

Situational pressures like these seem to affect women in particular for a variety of reasons. First, there are some obvious factors: persistent social expectations that women will accommodate the demands of childcare and family support. Partly, that's biological: child-rearing may be a shared responsibility but childbearing isn't. Second, some of these pressures arise because women often play a range of different roles outside work – as partner, parent, provider and community or family 'prop' – each of which can affect the range of work choices open to them. These varied roles increase the demands on their time, but recent research suggests that they are also a source of energy and meaning, so women often *want* their working lives to accommodate them (Ruderman *et al*, 2002). Third, women still encounter barriers and obstacles in the workplace, which affect the choices they make about their working lives. Creating a level playing field is not a once-and-done task but a regular challenge that women have to meet head-on, sometimes with significant consequences for their own career plans. Even those pressures which everyone faces may have a disproportionate effect on women: the economic need to work, whether you are a parent or not, to provide for yourself and others, both now and in the future, coping with whatever happens, such as divorce, illness or market downturns. And the lengthening of working lives hasn't always helped women in the workplace. As women age, society's perceptions of the work women can and should be doing impinges more on their choices than it does on men's choices. It shouldn't be so, and it isn't always so, but there are obvious examples: female actors who find work drying up when they reach 40, female mining engineers who are perceived as being not strong enough to work in inhospitable conditions, marketing specialists who are seen as too old to be able to handle social media marketing because they look like the 'wrong' generation.

In the midst of all these changing situations, most people want work which fits with their interests and skills. We are all driven by the things we want to do, even if we are sometimes constrained by some of the situations we find ourselves in. This book will also be useful for women like Isabel, as we shall see in the case study below, who is starting out on her working life and has fewer situational constraints but some strong interests which she wants to explore.

CASE STUDY   Looking for rewarding work

By the end of most weeks, Isabel is exhausted. She loves her job, working for the director of a small arts foundation. It's her first job and one she was delighted to get, since competition for jobs in the arts world is fierce. It's not well paid, though, since this sector is not known for its generous salary levels: the satisfaction is supposed to compensate for the low pay. And this will become an issue for her: she lives in an expensive city and has to pay off her student loan. She's doing well at work – her employers have recognized her abilities and given her more and more responsibility. But that isn't why she looks so tired.

'I'm out three nights a week working as a volunteer with a local theatre company, designing the sets and lighting rigs for various productions. I love it, crawling about backstage after a day at the office.' Some of her friends are incredulous – why do all that work, for no pay, given that she really does need the money? But Isabel knows exactly why: she yearns to do something more creative and her day job doesn't give her enough opportunity. Combining the two is one solution to the problem of doing work that you love, while still paying the rent. But there are mornings when she wonders whether she can keep up this level of activity. Is there some other way to build a more manageable, enjoyable and remunerated working life? Other than taking on two jobs simultaneously?

These stories of Lucy, Julie and Isabel illustrate the particularly complex blend of the situational and the personal which shape women's career choices at different stages of their lives. The constraints may be different, and their interests which drive them varied, but the challenge of finding work that feels successful is the same. And rising to that challenge requires navigational skill. Although everyone needs that skill, it's particularly important for women. We need to use it often and the waters we navigate are sometimes very turbulent. Equipping yourself with a clear strategy, setting out your direction, your purpose and your strengths, will help you. That's why this book is essentially a navigation handbook for women who work: it is not just a set of exercises to do once, but a review-and-explore process that you will probably need to revisit again and again, as the working world changes and you do, too.

Acknowledgements

If there's a book you really want to read, but it hasn't been written yet, then you must write it.
Toni Morrison, in a speech to the Ohio Arts Council, 1981

I wrote this book because there have been times in my working life when it was clear to me that my work just wasn't working. Not for me, not for my employers, not for my family. And I couldn't find quite the right book to help me. But in developing and testing the ideas in this book, I've benefited from support, challenge and insight from many women, and this is my chance to thank them.

I am very grateful to Gillian, Jessica, Jody, Yvonne, Jill, Alison, Sian, Sue, Andromachi, Joana, Robyn, Alison, Marella, Piyali, Sukh, Rosie, Alice, Margaret, Sally, Stephanie, Tracey, Cara, Clare, Melissa, Jhumar, Nazneen, Amy, Eliza, Wanda, June, Jan, Isobel, Clare, Claire, Janice, Phyllida, Sally, Liz, Josie, Kate, Kathryn, Frances, Fiona, Gillian, Jean, Jenny, Ceri, Rebecca, Catrin, Jo, Lucy, Melissa, Emma, Ruth, Mary, Leasil, Elaine, Elan, Sue, Andrea, Carlota, Aniela, Paula, Barbara, Usha, Sue, Virginia, and all the women who have been part of the Women Transforming Leadership programme at the University of Oxford. My thanks to you all: I've learned from you and so enjoyed your company and your conversation.

There are two women whose advice has been vital in writing this book: Alison Jones, at Practical Inspiration Publishing, who helped me shape it and get started, and Rebecca Bush, who helped me to get it over the finish line. Thank you both so much. I'm also grateful to the team at Kogan Page for all their effort and expertise.

Finally, thanks to you, the reader. I hope this book is as helpful to you as the ideas have been to me in my working life. That's what really matters.

Introduction

*What this book covers, why it will help,
and how to use it*

More than 10 years ago, I was working with a colleague, one of the most expert teachers of organizational and corporate strategy, in a classroom with a group of company leaders thinking about the future of their business. In the middle of the discussion, he turned to the group and said: 'By the way, do you have a strategy for you? If you don't, you should.' That was a key moment for me: the realization that I could use organizational strategy tools on myself, to make my own map, and plan my next steps. This proven process would help me to answer a whole range of questions about what I should do next and where I wanted to go. Since that day, I have been repurposing the most useful strategy tools which are taught in business schools to help individual women with their working lives.

That's the idea here: what works for an organization could work for you too. After all, organizations have the same navigation challenges as working people do: they have to find markets in which to use their resources to best effect. There are many strategy tools which they use and which are taught in business schools, but this book contains a selection which will work for you as an individual. I've tested these ideas in teaching groups of both male and female executives over the last decade, but the selection in this book is designed to work particularly well for women. The approach we'll take reflects the fact that women typically play multiple roles in their lives at work and outside, and that their working strategy absolutely has to accommodate the other responsibilities which they carry. And our roles change over time: the strategy which works for one phase of a woman's life may not work for another phase. A young woman in her twenties with few family obligations but a big student debt to pay off can take a different strategic approach to her working life compared with a woman in her forties whose partner's relocation means that she needs to find something remunerative to do while she helps her family settle in to their new life in a new country. The situations are different and so the strategy needs to be different, too.

What this book covers

There are several key concepts in this book. The main one is the idea that corporate strategy can usefully be applied to individuals; this is the basis for the whole book, and Chapter 1 will give an overview of the process and how it might work for you.

But before we start the strategy work, there are three other concepts which are worth unpacking briefly: the particular focus on your *working* life and your career; the definitions of success; and the idea of a map which you make yourself.

Working lives and 'careers'

First, you can tell from the title that this book will focus on your working life, but not exclusively. Because, of course, your working life is a part of the whole of your life. The phrase 'work–life balance' seems to ignore that fact: the subliminal suggestion is that you have a life outside work and then you have the other stuff you have to do, called work, which is somehow not part of your life. This doesn't seem a helpful idea. There are obviously some people whose work is solely devoted to providing funds for their exciting life outside work, but that's probably not you if you are reading this book. The idea that work is the servant of one's real life outside work doesn't gel with the way most of us split our time. After all, we often spend most of the daylight hours either at work or travelling to and from work, probably for at least five out of seven days a week.

In the search for equilibrium, I find it much more helpful to talk about 'work–home balance'. Although the focus of the book is on working lives, it's not sensible to ignore the other parts of our lives. This is especially true for women who work, since many of us play multiple roles and have other responsibilities outside our paid work. One of the simpler exercises to get you started asks you to think about the time you spend in the different areas of your life and, second, how well you feel you are doing in each of them. So we won't ignore these other areas of life, but they aren't our focus.

This book uses the word 'career' because, when we talk about working lives, we are not just envisaging a random series of different jobs. The word 'career' used to imply the idea that your working life is like a ladder: you start on the bottom rung and move up step by step over time. That may have been true in the past, for men if not for women, but it's not usually true now. Almost no one starts a job in their early twenties and progresses smoothly through the organization until they are offered a gold watch and a retirement party. In fact, working lives can sometimes feel more like 'careering' down a ski slope than progressing up through a series of sequential jobs as part of our carefully planned 'career'. But even when we are buffeted by organizational and economic change, the benefits of having a strategy are worth the effort. In fact, especially so.

Organizations sometimes say that there is no point in planning any more because the market is too turbulent, but what that really means is that the kind of planning they do has to change. And that's true for women who work, too. Less detailed step-by-step planning and more direction setting. More clarity about what we have to offer and where it might be most valuable. More about what we want to achieve and won't compromise on, and more ability to respond to opportunities. In fact, more strategy and a different kind of planning. So, in this book, the word 'career' is meant to express the idea of thoughtful progression through the journey of a working life.

Definitions of success

'Success' is the aim of your strategy work, but this book makes no assumptions about how you choose to define it. Success means different things to different people. It might even mean different things to you at different stages of your life. For example, in the early years of your working life, you might measure your success through promotion and pay, increasing responsibility and profile. At a later stage, when you have small children perhaps, success might mean having interesting and remunerative work which still allows you to get to the school plays and sports days. Maybe at a different stage, successful work might allow you time to develop a new hobby or to build up a new skill which might turn into work for the future. Or perhaps it's about a legacy, giving something back through mentoring, teaching or writing. For some women, success simply means financial security from their work.

Whatever it means for you, building your strategy around a clear definition will help you to achieve it. Why do we need a strategy to do this? Maybe you don't if you have a very straightforward definition of success. Marcus Buckingham asserts that there is one thing you need to know to ensure personal success: 'Discover what you don't like doing and stop doing it' (Buckingham, 2008). And he's not entirely wrong, as we discuss in Chapter 7 on using your strengths. The trouble is that for many people in the 21st century – and maybe for women in particular – it's not just about whether we like doing something or not. If only it were always that simple.

Women who feel that their working life is successful talk about work that is enjoyable, productive, meaningful and manageable, as well as rewarding. They have found work which literally 'works for them' in this current phase of their lives. It feels easy to get up in the morning for the interesting day ahead; they like their team and the effort they put in feels worthwhile. They can see the difference their work makes to customers, stakeholders or those who use the organization's services. They believe that their work also works for their employer, too. They come home at the end of most days feeling that they made a difference and, in the language of business schools, created some value.

It sounds good, doesn't it? It seems well worth the effort of devising a strategy for that kind of outcome.

Making a map

Although this is a book about strategy, we use the idea of the map to remind ourselves that we are setting out a direction to help us navigate to a destination. That idea helps anchor the thinking about strategy at the right level; it's not just a visualization of the ideal job as an end point, but about how to get there, often in turbulent conditions. You'll probably have to change course at times or even find another route. And your map will serve as a tool to orient yourself in getting from one point to another.

But maps are also about stories: ways of describing not just where we are, but *who* we are and how we got here. That sounds like a very metaphorical claim but the history of cartography is rich and varied – there are all kinds of maps, not just those to get you from A to B. There are maps which were prepared as tools to manage estates and empires, showing boundaries and areas of ownership, not just routes by land and water. Some maps show significance and proximity rather than actual physical distances, and that's an idea we will use in Chapter 2. And some maps show what could be, as well as what is already, deliberately mixing real cities with imaginary countries. Maps for military exercises mix real topography with hypothetical targets. There are psychographic maps, showing real countries located near religious conceptions of the locations of heaven and hell. Maps can be used to illustrate voting patterns or even the predominance of particular buzzwords. And there are spiritual maps, designed to guide the believer through this world to the next, providing a direction for their endeavours.

So the idea of a map is not just a metaphor. In making your own map, you will be documenting your understanding of the things that really matter to you and those aspects of your world which affect your working life – such as your responsibilities to your family, friends and community outside work, or a particular hobby or pastime to which you are committed. Maps are selective representations, and the map-maker has to make choices of what to include and what to leave out, so you'll be prioritizing as part of your strategy work. Finally, at the end of the strategy process you'll turn the map into a plan of action, to help you decide which route to take next, what to do, and what not to do.

Map-making in this sense is a really useful skill in a changing world. Since maps are simplified snapshots of a situation at a moment in time, they have to be remade every so often, because the world changes and you change too. You might even decide that you want to go somewhere different, because your definition of success has changed.

Why this book will help

This book is designed as a handbook to help you think clearly and strategically about your working life and your next step, whenever you need to do so. It brings together some tested strategy models and ideas from the business world, along with the stories of women who have used them. Over the last decade,

I have taught this strategy process to more than 300 women (and some men, too), working with them as they used it to make their own maps of their past, present and future working lives. But you might still be wondering why you need to go through a formal process. And it's true that there are other approaches to the idea of career development in books and blogs. For example, one approach involves asking yourself, 'What do I want out of life?' or 'What is my passion?' These are good questions: the trouble is that even if you can find the answer, it's not obvious how to turn it into action. A second approach focuses on engaging the imagination by visualizing your ideal working future. But there is a growing body of research that suggests that the visualization rarely turns into reality. The dreaming itself may do actual harm, because it's a form of mental escapism which can distract you from focusing on getting stuff done in the real world (Wiseman, 2009). It may make you less prepared for the real obstacles and setbacks which you encounter as you navigate through the changing working world. And many visualization exercises ask us to imagine what we might *be* in the future, and the static nature of the fantasy image is not helpful; by contrast, perhaps visualizing what you might *do* in the future and seeing yourself clearly doing it might be more useful. But not as useful as formulating a strategy and then implementing it.

So by reading this book, and going through the process it offers, you'll get two useful outcomes. First, you'll have a strategy, a clearer idea of what kind of work would work for you and how you might find it. The final two chapters of this book will help you turn these insights into action, because without some kind of implementation plan, your strategy is simply a map for a journey which you won't take.

Second, you'll develop the ability to reuse this strategy process whenever you need to. When market conditions change, or when the results of your current strategy aren't what you hoped for, you have to review and redo your strategy. When that happens – as it certainly will – you can come back to this process, or to parts of it, to remake your map.

How to use this book

This book works in the same way that a career strategy session in a classroom would work: taking you through the ideas in a particular sequence, the reasons why they might be useful to you, and providing an exercise in which you apply each idea to your own situation. The book is clearly structured and has plenty of subheadings so that you can easily find what you need. Most women have more than enough to do in life, and this strategy process needs to be as efficient as possible! To that end, the chapters all follow the same format, to make it easier to navigate.

But the structure is also designed to signal to you that you can pick and choose the parts that are useful for you. You absolutely don't have to read every section of every chapter. You might want to look at each of the chapter headings and the question it poses in sequence, but every chapter also contains other material that you may or may not want to read, depending on what you want to get out of the book. So here is a summary of each of the standard sections in each chapter and what they offer you, just to help you to use the book and the process it describes in a way that suits you.

Each chapter starts with the **question** you might want to answer at this stage of your strategy review; these are obvious and useful questions and the chapter is intended to help you generate some answers. Strategy work proceeds by asking the right questions to focus your thinking and then answering them through analysis and reflection.

Just in case you need to be convinced that the question really is useful, there is a section which I've called '**why this matters to you**'. This amplifies the reasons why the question is helpful in the strategy process and what you might get out of the chapter and the exercise.

Each chapter contains an **idea**, a concept or framework to help you think strategically about your working life. Most of these are drawn from traditional corporate strategy, but three of them are taken from psychology and organizational development.

Then there is a section which explains the **parallels with corporate strategy**, comparing and contrasting what an organization might do with this idea and what you might do with it. These sections explain the corporate pedigree for the idea and you can skip them if you wish. But you might find that there is something useful there, too, for the organization you work with rather than just for your own career strategy. One of the women I worked with subsequently wrote to me to say that the model she had found most useful for her own forward planning – the Purpose Alignment model in Chapter 6 – had also been extremely useful for her at work. She had been asked to set up a new division in the company and she had used the model with her team to help structure themselves around their new purpose.

The section that follows sets out some of the **underlying research** on each topic. This section anchors the idea or its application in well-researched theory and contains some related ideas that might stimulate your thinking. If you are keen to get to the exercise, though, you could also skip this section, or come back to it later.

Each chapter also contains a series of **case studies** and **stories** of women like us who have wrestled with particular issues and have been helped by using the idea and doing the exercise. These stories are sprinkled throughout the text because some readers find the real examples more helpful than theory, but if they don't work for you, you can move past these case studies – they are clearly indicated to allow you to do just that.

And finally, in each chapter there is an **exercise**. This is an opportunity for you to do some structured reflection, with some guidance gleaned from corporate strategy processes. The exercises are entirely optional, of course – but I would encourage you to have a go if you can, because they will be useful to you if you can find the time to do them.

And I mean really do them, not just read through the instructions. There is some interesting new research that compares what happens to the brain when someone plays the piano as opposed to merely *thinking* about playing the piano. Rather surprisingly, brain activity is similar in both situations: some parts of the brain fire up even when you just think about piano playing. But it's not quite the same: if you can actually do the exercises, you will be rewarded with insight somewhere along the way. It might not arrive immediately, but the experience of working with these exercises over the last decade indicates that everyone finds some new insight if they put the time aside to do them.

That's why there is an example **worksheet** at the end of most chapters, based on the diagram in each chapter which helps explain the idea or model. This worksheet offers a way to structure your thoughts and to encourage you to capture your insights, but you don't have to use it – if it doesn't suit you, simply use a piece of paper.

Every chapter also contains **extension ideas**, designed either to help you to develop your work on the exercise or to offer some ideas for implementation tactics which you could take along the way. There is also a simple **summary** at the end of every chapter to serve as an anchor for each stage of your work. And there are references and suggestions for further reading at the end of the book.

Use your instinct

Strategy processes in organizations often involve enormous amounts of data collection and analysis and can be so structured that they feel onerous and restrictive. Here, too, the exercises will encourage you to gather some data and analyse what you find, think about alternatives, and maybe even do some experimentation. If that sounds rather daunting or too formal, too much like a corporate strategy exercise, don't worry: this a process about *you*, the subject you know best, and so there are no rules, only some guidelines and suggestions. Your instinct will be your best guide and you may well want to choose parts of the process which help you right now. When I teach this material at the Women Transforming Leadership programme at Oxford, we use a combination of quiet individual reflection and conversations over coffee with someone who is also trying the same exercise. And most people find this kind of personal strategizing fun and very enlightening.

SUMMARY

- This is a book about the journey to successful work, however you choose to define that. It focuses on your career, your working life and how you want it to progress.

- There's a particular navigation challenge in finding work that works and feels successful. Although almost all men and women face this challenge, typically women will face it more frequently.

- This is the same kind of challenge which organizations face in navigating changing markets. They develop corporate strategies which set out how they will make the most of their resources and opportunities. What works for them works for individuals too. This book is about the application of corporate strategy tools and ideas to help you develop your own strategy for your working life.

- The book uses the idea of a map: setting out where you want to get to, and how you plan to get there.

- Success at work means different things to different people, but it could be defined as finding the right job, at the right time in your life, when you have the right skills to do the job, in an organizational context which suits you. Those four dimensions – job, time, skills and organizational context – have to be in sync to be sustainably successful. That's why it's not easy to find that kind of job, and why it helps to have a strategy.

What's next?

The next chapter outlines the strategy process and the ideas in the rest of the book, so that you can see how this will help you to make your own map.

CHAPTER ONE

Devising a strategy for you: the Strategy Triangle

What sort of strategy process will work best for you?

This chapter will give you an overview of the process set out in this book to make your own map, constructing your strategy for you. We'll draw the comparison with corporate strategy, looking at what strategy is and how it's formulated, but we'll focus on the way this will work for you as an individual.

Why this matters to you

During any strategy process, we aim to find the answers to some important questions. Where am I trying to get to? What shall I do next? How shall I get there? These are the right questions, but although they are easy to ask, they are usually very hard to answer. There are so many aspects to consider and the answers are likely to have a huge impact on the future. So any strategy process has to be both broad and rigorous – and that's why organizations pay so much attention to it. And that's also why there are so many strategy tools, taught in business schools and published in business books.

So, what sort of process will work best for you? This chapter answers that question, with an overview of a strategy process that works for individuals. Subsequent chapters contain a selected set of ideas, models and exercises to help you. Some of them may appeal to you more than others and some will have particular relevance for you. Some may look as if they won't be as helpful to you at the present, but they might still be worth trying, because they'll help you see your working life from a different perspective.

The idea

Strategy is one of those words which is used all the time but which means different things to different people. It is often part of the job description of senior leaders – its origins in the Greek word *strategos,* meaning a military leader, clearly connects it with leadership.

Formulating strategy is about setting a direction for the organization or entity as it moves forward. It implies taking action to create its future rather than simply arriving at tomorrow. Strategy is also about story – the narrative about where we are trying to get to, and why. Strategic decisions can be large or small in scale, and can encompass the short, medium and long term. This set of definitions underlines the point: strategy formulation can be complicated, so the clearer and more straightforward the process the better.

FIGURE 1.1 The Strategy Triangle

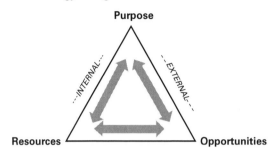

Adapted from Professor Marcus Alexander's Strategy Triangle

The three elements of strategy

When we talk about strategy, the conversation covers three different elements: purpose; resources and skills; and external opportunities. One of the most brilliant strategy professors I know, Professor Marcus Alexander, uses this diagram to represent these three elements of strategy.

The diagram reminds us that in formulating strategy, you need to generate insights about all three elements. But you also need to understand the links and interactions between them and keep the three in balance. As an introduction to our strategy process, let's look at each aspect.

Much strategy work focuses on articulating where you are aiming to get to; this is sometimes called the 'vision' or 'mission' school of strategy. You may have worked in an organization with a framed vision statement on the wall, listing its aims, beliefs and values. These statements have been a long-standing business fad and may motivate some people. But one definition of 'vision' is 'an unreal dream' or 'a supernatural apparition', and, over time, these framed statements can grow stale. That's why we will talk about purpose, rather than vision. Purpose statements articulate what you are for and why, and if they are clear enough, they help to generate the kind of implementable strategy which will lead to sustained success.

The second aspect of strategy is resources: the skills and capabilities you have and the time and energy you want to devote to your working life. In organizational terms, that's about the people in the organization and the other resources that the organization possesses, such as money, time, information, equipment or even reputation. Of course, these resources can be developed or acquired – for example, when an organization acquires another business, or invests in hiring new staff with key skills. For us as individuals, the development of our skills is an obvious part of implementing our strategy, but there are various options for how we might do this and what to focus on – and that, too, is a part of our strategy.

The third aspect is the external focus on possible opportunities which the organization could respond to and thus generate value and deliver good results. The link between this aspect and the other two is important: all three should be logically aligned. In other words, the ideal opportunity is one which is in line with your purpose and for which you have the right resources. Business school strategy lectures sometimes appear to emphasize this external aspect over the others, partly because it's the least controllable. Some strategy processes involve enormous amounts of market analysis because new opportunities may suddenly arise which may not be part of the original purpose. Take a business example: a UK bookseller was originally set up to sell niche or hard-to-find books but grew into a major player in the Australian market by spotting an opportunity. Even though they had no physical presence there, they identified an opportunity in the Australian tax regime on book pricing: books sent into Australia from abroad attracted no tax and were therefore cheaper to buy. Spotting opportunities like this and capitalizing on them allowed them to become one of the fastest growing booksellers in Europe.

This idea of seizing the opportunity is relevant to us as individuals, too. If you suddenly get a surprising phone call from a headhunter or recruitment consultant about a job which you would not normally consider or didn't even know existed, take the call – it might be worth it. Sometimes it leads to a new and very successful route. There's an important point about strategy here: it's not a rigid constraint, with a plan set in concrete, but an iterative process which helps you to respond successfully to the constant changes in your life and your world.

The Strategy Triangle diagram is also a good way of illustrating what might happen if the three elements get out of balance. The neat equilateral triangle might be warped and distorted, with some obvious pitfalls. For example, too much focus on the external opportunities might cause an organization to spread its resources on a range of activities which are not core to its business. The point is the same for individuals: although an opportunity-led career strategy seems increasingly common in a turbulent, fast-changing marketplace, it has some risks. New opportunities might arise which seem fascinating and worth exploring, but they might also take you down a cul-de-sac in career terms which could be hard to escape.

Equally, organizations which are too internally focused spend management time and energy on internal change programmes which take so long that they miss the very market opportunity they were trying to address. That's true for individuals too: all development is beneficial, but if you can't use what you learn on a development programme or training course, your new skills will fade over time and won't pay off in terms of progress and achievement at work. Finally, an excessive focus on a tightly defined purpose or aim might make an organization rule out some interesting new opportunities which it could easily benefit from – and that's true for us, too.

So the message of the Strategy Triangle is that the three elements are interlinked, and a change in one aspect will cause change in at least one other aspect, too. Here's an example of this in Nina's story.

CASE STUDY New skills, new opportunity, new direction

When she was promoted to operations team leader at an international gas company, Nina discovered that her new role meant that she spent most of her time working with the IT department. That hadn't been in the job description! Every time there was a new systems development project, she was the person assigned to work on it, because she really understood the operational processes. 'The trouble was,' she told me, 'that I didn't know much about technology. It's boring to have to ask for explanations all the time, and I felt like I was always one step behind. It wasn't that enjoyable.' So, almost as an experiment, and without telling anyone, she booked herself onto an introductory 'learn to code' weekend. 'I was very surprised – it was quite interesting! And I could do it!' Of course, this still didn't solve the problem at work, so she signed up for a longer online programme, covering the fundamentals of both IT and coding. 'That really helped. After about 18 months, I knew enough about the field – or at least felt that I did – to hold my own in meetings. I got on better with team members, and I think we made better decisions because we had clearer discussions.' And Nina's new skills opened up a new opportunity for her: she was invited to apply for a more senior role in the IT team as a business analyst. It had never been part of her plan to move out of front-line operations, but the more she explored this new opportunity, the more interesting it seemed. So, when she was offered the job, she took it – and that took her career in a completely new direction.

Keeping the three elements of the Strategy Triangle in balance is a necessary part of strategy formulation, but it's also useful in action planning. If you can see the implications of a change in one aspect, you can also see what else needs to change, and plan accordingly. Here's a hypothetical example: if you suddenly develop an interest in becoming a sports commentator but you currently have neither the relevant skills nor any experience, then, at present, you have a dream rather than a strategy. And the way to turn the dream into more of a reality is obvious if you think about all three elements of the Strategy

Triangle: given this particular purpose, think about the opportunities that are out there to get work in the right kind of organization, and consider the resources – skills, energy, time, willingness to relocate, for example – which you might need to develop in order to devise a strategy which you can actually implement.

The connection between the three elements of the Strategy Triangle, with both the internal and external focus, will help you to organize your strategy thinking. It will help you decide what to do, as well as what not to do. Sometimes, it's absolutely the right strategic decision to say no to a new opportunity because it doesn't fit with the rest of your life and you don't want to make the required changes to accommodate it, given where you are now. To be realistic and implementable, strategy has to take into account the constraints under which you work. And the Strategy Triangle can help clarify your choices when situations change and new constraints arise. For example, if you suddenly find that you have to work part-time for a while because of a family issue, in effect your resources have changed because now you have less time to devote to your paid work. So you might find that you need to look for a different kind of opportunity. And perhaps your purpose might also need to alter. Maybe for the next few years your strategy is less about paid progression to senior management and more about finding something relatively interesting and remunerated which allows you enough time and energy to meet your other responsibilities outside work.

Parallels with corporate strategy

Most of the ideas in this book come from mainstream strategy work. They are used by organizations of all kinds from all over the world to help them navigate changing circumstances, to make the best use of their resources in line with their purpose.

Their employees want to know what lies ahead and so they have to make a map for their future.

Given how many strategy frameworks and models there are, one of the first questions an organizational strategy team has to answer is: which strategy approach shall we use? Often the choice of the approach is driven by current fashion – what's being written about in blogs and taught at business schools. Or it might be a choice based on previous experience, to reuse the same set of tools and approaches which the team used last time. There is no one strategy tool which is right for all situations, and a combination of different approaches is more likely to generate clearer thinking and therefore a more successful strategy.

Using organizational strategy ideas for an individual is not such an unusual idea as it might seem; after all, strategy itself was originally developed in a military context to help with campaign planning and, in that sense, it has already been repurposed to apply to a commercial and business context. As markets opened up and developed in the 20th century, particularly in the USA, leaders – who may themselves have had a military background – began to use strategy tools as part of business planning. So you could say that we are simply repurposing these tools again, to apply to each of us as individuals rather than to the organizations we work in.

But because we are working on individual strategy, this book does include three other useful ideas from elsewhere. One is from psychology – the Strengths model in Chapter 7 – because part of any individual strategy is about self-development. The second comes from philosophy – the Ikigai model in Chapter 4 – because this is a book about changing your thinking as well as about devising a strategy. And the third uses a creative technique to help you articulate the fundamental strategic concept of purpose. Although these three are not classic strategy models, they are sometimes used by strategy teams as part of their process, and you'll find them useful as part of your strategy process.

The underlying research

Strategy theory and practice are built around mental models – ideas, concepts and frameworks – which are ways of thinking about the present and future in order to answer key questions about direction and objectives. These strategy tools and ideas are what academics call 'heuristics' – that is, tools for thinking. They don't contain the answers themselves but they are designed to help answer important questions. Techniques don't make strategy, but people do – and experience and evidence suggest that we can do it more effectively with some tools to help. One of my favourite quotations from Donald Norman in a book entitled *Things that Make Us Smart* sums this up: 'The power of the unaided mind is highly overrated... the real powers come from devising external aids that enhance cognitive abilities... Tools of thought... cognitive artifacts – that complement abilities and strengthen mental powers' (Norman, 1993).

These tools of thought offer a range of different perspectives. Some strategy models have a market and competitor focus, such as Porter's Five Forces model, and some are much more internal and operational, like those which look at internal re-engineering of the whole organization as a source of competitive advantage. Some span both internal and external, such as the SWOT analysis (Strengths, Weaknesses, Opportunities and Threats) or Value Chain analysis. In most situations, a combination of these is key to developing a workable strategy, as the Strategy Triangle illustrates.

The strategy models

So which techniques will you want to use in devising your own strategy? Here's an overview of the models and exercises in each of the succeeding chapters. This summary will give you an idea of the overall process as well as the key questions to be answered.

Strategy processes typically have three stages in order to answer three questions: Where am I now? Where do I want to go? How will I get there? This book uses the same structure.

Where am I now?

Stage 1 of the strategy process focuses on your current situation. The very first model, though, helps you to think about how you got to where you are now. Looking at the past may seem an odd place to start when what you really want to do is to devise a strategy for your future. But answering this question will give you a clearer sense of the resources and skills you have developed so far. That's helpful, since sometimes you realize you have resources which you aren't using fully and which could be more useful in the future. So, in Chapter 2, you'll be asked to draw the Journey Map of your working life, to answer the questions: '**How did you get to where you are now? What's the story of your working life so far?**'

In Chapter 3, there is a set of exercises designed to help you answer the question: '**What's working well for you in your working life right now and what are you less happy with?**' You'll consider balance and priorities in your life and exactly where you spend your time and energy right now. Maybe you are entirely happy with some of it, or perhaps it's not working as well as it might? Although you are laying the groundwork for your strategy work, you may find some immediate actions which you could take, right now, to make some improvements. Even in the middle of strategizing, some tactics become so obvious that you won't want to wait before taking action.

Where do I want to go?

In Stage 2, we turn our attention to your future, the destination you are going to aim for. There are four different models here, each of which will help you to envisage your ideal future in different ways. We start with a philosophical idea – Ikigai – to get you to think about *why* you do what you do. This will help you to answer the question: 'What kind of work do you see yourself doing as part of your successful working life?' Although Ikigai isn't a traditional strategy model, it covers the dimensions of the Strategy Triangle and will give you a different perspective on it.

Then, in Chapter 5, we look at the top point of the Strategy Triangle, to answer the question: 'What's the purpose you serve?' Sometimes, this idea of purpose can be hard to articulate, so this chapter uses a creative storytelling technique to help you clarify and express it.

In Chapter 6, we look at the internal dimension of the Strategy Triangle: the link between your purpose and your resources. This chapter will help you to find some answers to the important question: 'How can you organize your life around your purpose?' Business schools emphasize the importance of alignment between an organization's purpose and its resources, and it's just as vital for individuals.

Finally in this stage, in Chapter 7, we turn to one key part of your resources: your capabilities, skills and experiences. Most individual work on career strategy involves self-development at some point, and this chapter offers you a new way of answering the question: 'What's worth developing?' This chapter focuses on your strengths but will also help you to decide what you might do about those capabilities that are not so strong.

How will I get there?

Strategy formulation can be both demanding and interesting, but it's not really useful unless you can turn your insights into some kind of action. You have to make your strategy real. So in the final stage of your work, we'll look at transition planning, setting out your plans for getting from where you are now to where you want to be – and taking action.

Before we get into the grit of preparing and planning, Chapter 8 will help you to think broadly about the kind of transitions you might want to make, with one final strategy model to help you. This model is useful if your strategy work shows you that you want to make a major change at work – either in the role you do, or in the organization you work for, or both.

In Chapter 9, we come back to the Strategy Triangle to understand two different but complementary ways of implementing your strategy. Your preparation and planning work will involve thinking about what actions you want to take and how to take them. But the goal of strategy is not to create a single, perfect plan which you can then simply implement, step by step; that doesn't work for organizations and it won't work for individuals because work changes and so do we. Rather, the statement of direction which strategy work reveals to you requires a map: a navigational tool that you can use to help you adjust your course from time to time.

Those adjustments come through the tactical decisions and choices you make every day – and that's what the final chapter is about. Tactics are a key part of strategy implementation, not just because they are the actions which get us under way, but because they themselves are micro-strategies which deliver insight about where your strategy is working and where it isn't.

EXTENSION IDEAS

The extension ideas in every chapter give you the chance to expand your thinking on the specific exercise, or to start implementing your insights straightaway, before you've finished formulating your strategy. If you are an action-oriented person, you'll want to get started with doing something, and sometimes that's absolutely the right thing to do. But in some chapters, there are no suggestions for immediate actions because the insight developed in that particular chapter is only part of the answer. It needs to be added to the mix in your strategy before you start implementing it.

SUMMARY

- This chapter describes the process of formulating your own strategy for success and the content we'll cover.

- Typically, strategy processes go through three stages: examining the present (where are you now?), the ideal future (where do you want to get to?) and how to make the transition (how will you get there?).

- The content of strategy work – its scope and what it covers – is illustrated in the Strategy Triangle model: it illustrates the three elements of good strategy:
  - purpose;
  - resources – capabilities, time, energy;
  - opportunities – the external possibilities to explore or ignore.

- All three elements are linked and a successful strategy has to have a degree of coherence between the three, as the Strategy Triangle diagram illustrates. For example, if you have an ambition to achieve something but you have no relevant skills, you either need to take some action to develop those skills, or accept that your ambition is an unrealizable dream.

- This book uses the same structure as the strategy formulation process, with its three stages. In every chapter there is a particular model or idea, drawn from corporate strategy or from psychology or philosophy, to help you think clearly about your strategy.

- The model in each chapter is intended to help you generate insights about your ideal working life and the strategy to realize it. But you have to turn these insights into action: although you might identify some immediate steps to be taken as you go, the final two chapters will focus on planning and doing.

What's next?

Now that you have an overview of what's ahead, let's get under way.

Examining the past and present to plan for the future

This first stage of the strategy process does exactly what it says in the title. It gives you two different frameworks: one to look at your working life to date, and the second to examine your current situation. The exercises in Chapter 2 will help you to reflect on everything you've done and learned so far. Chapter 3 will help you to see how one key aspect of the Strategy Triangle is playing out in your current situation: how you are using your resources at work and outside. From these two exercises, you'll generate some insights to feed into your thinking about the future. These might be about something you want to keep – something which is working well right now, for example. Or they might be aspects that you definitely want to avoid in your map for the future.

CHAPTER TWO

How you got to where you are now: your Journey Map

What brought you here? What's the story of your working life so far? What were the key moments? And how has your career been progressing?

Why this matters to you

If you can take the time to set out the journey of your working life on paper, you'll find it gives you a fresh view of your career to date. Looking back, you'll see the high points, which might remind you of your achievements, as well as the low points, which will certainly show you how you've dealt with problems. You aren't aiming to recreate your CV; rather, you're literally drawing a map of the journey of your working life over time, thinking about what has happened and how you felt about it. We sometimes aren't conscious of all of the things we have done and dealt with – we don't quite know what we know. It's useful to remind ourselves of the skills we have developed and changes we have made in the past, as we start preparing for a new future. This is why this reflective idea can be particularly useful for women: it helps to raise your confidence when you see what you have already coped with and how far you have already come.

And there's one more reason for starting our strategy work here: this is also a useful exercise in mental preparation – limbering up, if you will – because, as neurological research tells us, 'focal, conscious, directed attention is necessary for the capture of explicit memory... and this is most significant for the creation of a coherent and consistent "story of the self"' (Chisholm, Swart and Brown, 2015).

This idea of the 'story of the self' is at the heart of strategy: even corporate strategy is about narrative. Being clear about your story, about what you have done as well as what you want to do, will help you in making decisions about your working life. The clearer you are, the better your decisions will turn out to be.

So although the exercise looks backwards, it is really preparation for looking forwards. You may already see the need for some changes – in other words, what got you here won't get you there. Or perhaps you feel you were happiest and most successful in a particular role or industry in the past and this is the time to reconsider that option for the future. Either way, this exercise will help you to develop the next chapter in the story of you by setting out in front of you the chapters of your story so far. It can be surprisingly helpful, as Abby found, in the case study below.

CASE STUDY   Should Abby apply?

The minute she saw the job advertisement, Abby was interested. She wasn't exactly unhappy in her current job, but this looked like a really interesting opportunity in a different organization. After 20 years working for a national distribution business, moving around from jobs in operations to roles in HR and back again, with a few years in the IT function, Abby was well-networked and valued by her boss and her team. Her job felt comfortable. And maybe just a little dull? But she was tired of travelling into central London each day, and the prospect of something different at this stage in her life was enticing. The advertisement described what would be a new role for her: setting up a project team to develop a new service offering, co-ordinating work across various functions, and working with digital specialists, operational managers and the finance department.

'So why don't you apply?' encouraged her friends.

'Well, it could be risky – it looks like a short-term job and we all know that these jobs can disappear when the project is over. And anyway, I have no experience of this kind of role – co-ordinating stuff. How would I do it? How would I persuade the interviewer that I could do it? Oh, and I would have to leave all my friends here, too…' Abby had almost convinced herself not to apply, but her friends suggested that she set out specifically what she was concerned about. So she wrote herself a list of questions: what experience do I have that might be relevant? How would I manage the transition to a completely new organization in which I wouldn't know anybody? How could I work with experts in the finance team, for example, given that I have no finance experience myself? How would I go about building new relationships? Abby knew that she would be asked questions like these at interview, if she got to that stage, but she also decided that if she couldn't come up with some good answers to convince herself, she wouldn't even apply. So rather than staring at her CV, she decided that the Journey Map exercise would give her a fresh view of her career so far, and might help answer these questions.

We'll come back to Abby's story later in this chapter, to see exactly how the exercise helped her.

The idea

The idea in this chapter is to make your own map of what you have done so far in your working life. The exercise will get you to draw the story of your working life so far in the form of a map with a timeline. It should cover the specific roles and jobs you have had, the events that have happened to you along the way, and also how you felt about them at each point. You'll see where new opportunities arose, and where you developed your skills, two key elements of the Strategy Triangle that we first saw in Chapter 1. Looking back at the past in this way helps you to be explicit about what you know, what you've learned and what you've achieved. Literally drawing this out on paper gets you away from the long-standing stories you may have been telling yourself about your working life. It might change your view of those stories and open up some new insights to feed in to your strategy for the future.

Parallels with corporate strategy

Organizational history can be viewed as a journey with particular phases, and this exercise is as useful in that context as it will be for you as an individual. Why? Because understanding what has happened previously is an important part of understanding what's happening now and – perhaps more importantly – *why* it's happening.

Here's a story to back up this point. Some years ago I was hired by an organization to lead a major change initiative sponsored by the new CEO. It looked like a good role: there was a clear sense of purpose, sufficient levels of funding and a reasonable timescale to achieve some significant changes in processes and structures. It turned out to be much more difficult than anyone expected, particularly for those of us who were new to the organization. We learned that, over the last nine years, this organization had appointed seven different CEOs, each one brought in with a brief to restructure the business – and each one had left the organization after about a year. Not one of the new leaders had achieved all their goals. As a result, the organization was full of people who were increasingly inured to new initiatives and change programmes; their view was 'Here is another one of those change projects, just like the last three or four. I think I will sit quietly and wait until this initiative passes, just like the last one and the one before that.'

In this situation, the most useful thing I could have done at the outset would have been to get a sense of how the organization had got to this point; I should have understood the story of the organization's journey. It wouldn't have been hard to guess how people were likely to react to yet another change programme if I had known this.

So, in corporate strategy, it can be very useful to see clearly what's happened in the past as a guide for future action. Every corporate journey is different, just as every individual journey is too. There are no right or wrong answers in this strategy exercise, but we have a better sense of the present context if we understand what's happened in the past. And we start to see what might work in the future, as well as what we have tried before that didn't work.

The underlying research

The research on corporate journeys of change reveals that, for every organization, there are some clearly identifiable phases, such as times of expansion or restructuring. But it also shows that there is no standard sequence, even within the same industrial sector (Ruddle, 1999). Organizations develop and grow in different ways and their journeys look different, even if their product range and market position might look very similar. The Journey Map idea is a useful reminder for organizational leaders that there is no recipe to follow – no standard set of right answers – and as we go into this exercise, it's a useful reminder for us, too.

It's interesting to see how organizations choose to define these phases; sometimes they are simply a function of the area of focus for the new developments (eg downsizing or expansion, acquisition or organic growth, a concentration on an existing market or a new product) and sometimes they are characterized by the personality of the senior leader. It also becomes obvious when looking at these journeys of change why leaders are sometimes fired – because the kind of leadership needed for the particular phase of the journey is not the kind that the current leader is able to provide. This is the second useful insight that organizations can find in using this lens to consider their history: given the phase we are in right now, what kind of leadership skills do we need? And what might we need as we go into the next phase?

There is some very new and emerging research from Oxford – not yet published at the time of writing – about the phases in women's working lives, which also underlines the utility of this journey idea. For example, if you have just moved into a new organization, perhaps into your first major leadership role, you might be quite focused on fitting in, understanding how the organization likes to work, trying to see what the accepted rules are for getting things done and being successful. The research into women's working lives suggests that this phase might be termed one of 'compliance and alignment'; we all might find ourselves in this kind of phase at various times. The idea of different phases can help to orient us and guide what we choose to concentrate on at any given time. And it's a useful reminder that, whenever we change organizations, no matter how senior or successful, we will probably have to go through this 'finding out and fitting in' phase.

During research interviews, women also tell stories about particular moments in their working lives. They often talk about the time when they finally accepted themselves as a working woman and as a leader, and, from that point on, consciously chose to manage their working life accordingly, to own their working lives. Sometimes these were moments of crisis, or sometimes of a sudden and significant step up, but they appear in our lives as 'crucible' moments and we come out of them changed in some way.

Was there a moment like this for you? Preparing your Journey Map might reveal to you exactly when this was – or how many such moments you have had and how you changed as a result.

The exercise: guidance

The Journey Map is a picture of your working life so far, drawn as a graph with two axes. The horizontal axis for your graph is time, probably beginning at the date you started your first job and running to the present, marked in single years. This level of detail will help make sure that you recall what happened and what you did as clearly as possible.

Step 1: What does success mean to you?

The vertical axis is for you to define. Often, people choose to define it as 'success' – whatever that might mean to them. Perhaps it means promotions, pay rises, awards or accolades, the external signs of a successful career which other people notice. Or you might focus much more on your own sense of satisfaction at work, or happiness. Some people choose to measure their success in terms of contribution, either to their employer or to their community. Occasionally, people choose a much simpler definition, focusing on one particular thing that matters to them, such as financial security, for instance.

As we begin the exercise, choose the definition of success that seems most useful and comfortable to you. This is *your* Journey Map, and it needs to reflect your working life. But don't worry too much about the definition you choose – your first, most instinctive thought is usually the right one to work with at the outset. When you become more familiar with this exercise, you may want to

FIGURE 2.1   Your definition of success – the vertical axis

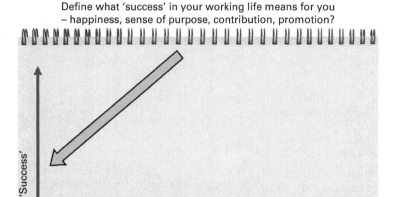

Your Journey Map
Define what 'success' in your working life means for you
– happiness, sense of purpose, contribution, promotion?

change the definition, or even draw more than one map using external definitions of success as well as internal ones. This model is designed to be a tool for thinking, and you may at some point want to customize the tool to help you to think more clearly.

Step 2: What are the key moments in your working life so far?

The first things to plot on your map are those key moments in your working life when something significant happened. Many of these incidents will be obvious, and you will remember them easily: your first job, your first promotion, the changes in your role at work, or times when you moved to a new job with a new employer. You will probably recall many of them with pleasure because they were times when something positive happened. But there are also the moments you would perhaps rather not remember, such as missing out on a promotion or not getting that new

FIGURE 2.2 Key moments

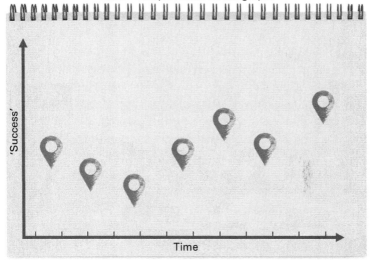

Adding key moments to your map

Identify the key moments in your working life – transitions, high points, crises – and plot them on the graph.

job. These less successful moments are an important part of your journey and so they, too, need to be marked on the map.

For most people, the Journey Map will include between four and eight key moments; if you find around that number, the exercise will work well. If you have fewer than four key moments, you might want to look at your CV again. Try to identify some other moments that are perhaps less immediately obvious while still being important. For example, you might want to include times when your role changed – such as the point when you first started to supervise other people, taking on a team leadership role. Your list might also include being made redundant, or a development programme or training course which made a difference to the way you work. If you have more than 10 moments or incidents, you might want to group some of them together, or shorten the timescale of your map, to focus on particular phases of your working life.

All these moments anchor your map. Capture a short description of each one so that the progress of your journey is clear.

CASE STUDY Ann's key moments

Ann worked for a financial services company in the Midlands for nearly 10 years. Things had mostly gone well; she'd been promoted twice and had moved into some interesting project roles working on new developments. But during a large and stressful merger project, she had a major disagreement with her boss, culminating in a very tetchy final meeting. And as she drove home from that meeting, she knew that she couldn't continue in this role. Her employers then asked her to move to the London head office, to take up a new role, presumably to get her out of the current situation. But when she declined, because she didn't want to uproot the family, she was made redundant. Her Journey Map also showed her first job offer after that point – a similar job in the same

FIGURE 2.3 Ann's Journey Map

Ann's Journey Map

Ann's Journey Map shows her two promotions, and then the disagreement with her boss – together with the subsequent redundancy – as key events. It also shows her first job offer after that point; this was a similar job in the same industry, which was reassuring for her, but which she declined.

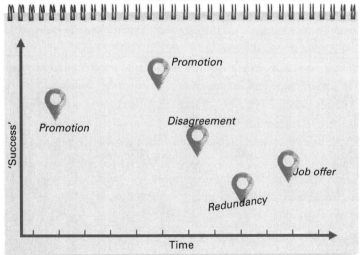

industry – which, after much heart-searching, she also declined. 'I wondered whether I was an idiot to turn this job down, but I'd realized that I wanted to do something completely different, not simply to do the same job but for a different employer. I also remember being very anxious about saying no, but looking back, it was a key moment. That decision put me on a different course.'

Step 3: How are the key moments connected in your Journey Map?

Your working life has obviously been more than just a set of key moments, and the Journey Map needs to reflect what happened in between those moments, and how one led to another. If you draw on the map a line that reflects how successful you felt yourself to be as you moved from one key moment to the next, you are literally drawing your journey.

FIGURE 2.4 Linking key moments

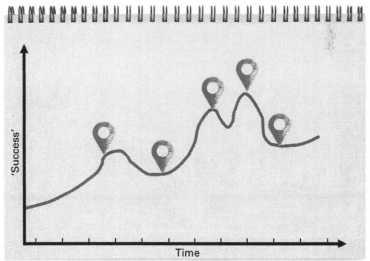

Linking key moments

Draw the line which links those key moments reflecting your 'success' as it changed and developed.

For most of us, the connecting line is neither straight nor neat and doesn't move evenly from one level of success to the next. Like a country lane, it meanders from moment to moment, some successful, some less so. We all have this kind of pattern in our working lives and it is completely normal.

As you draw on the map, you will see that this exercise is not like joining the dots, since sometimes your sense of 'success' fluctuates without there being a key moment to precipitate the change. For example, here's what Clare's Journey Map revealed.

CASE STUDY Clare's journey: moving on after a triumph

In Clare's Journey Map, the early stages of her working life progressed smoothly from promotion to promotion, from one organization to a series of larger and more successful companies. As

FIGURE 2.5   Clare's Journey Map

Clare's Journey Map

After a steady progression at work, Clare's sense of success reached a peak when she moved to a new role. But her lack of satisfaction in the job increased and her working relationship with her new boss got worse, and this exercise helped her to realize that she would have to take some action.

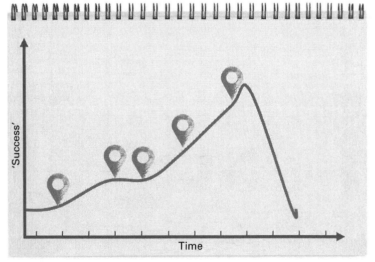

she said, 'In my twenties, I thought that this was what my working life would always be: interesting work, growing confidence, and learning new skills. And when I was 32, I was assigned to a new high-profile team, to work on a brand new product for the business – and I thought that proved the point. But in reality this new role was much less satisfying than I thought it would be, and my boss had a completely different approach to work from mine. It was a shock for me to come up against these difficulties – and you can see on my Journey Map the huge drop in my morale.' After struggling to improve things for more than a year, Clare finally acknowledged to herself that it was time to make a move. Maybe going back to her previous role, or leaving the organization completely. As the Journey Map reminded her, she had made changes like this before and could probably do so again. That was just enough encouragement to get started on answering the question: 'What next?'

Step 4: Are there other key moments to add?

Now that you have drawn the journey from moment to moment, you may be reminded of some additional key moments which you hadn't previously considered. If your map shows a time when your sense of success changed – for the better or for the worse – but that appears unconnected with a key moment, you might want to think back to see if there was a particular event which might have caused the change. Recognizing a new key moment is a very useful outcome – sometimes, what seemed unimportant at the time was actually an inflection point.

But there is no need to add anything if you feel that the diagram you have drawn reflects your working life fairly accurately. Unimportant detail won't necessarily assist you in future planning. In this exercise, as with the others in this book, your instinct for what matters to you is a good guide.

Step 5: What has happened in your life outside work?

Although the focus of this exercise – and this book – is on your working life, the Journey Map might be even more useful if it reflects what has happened in your life outside work. Our working lives are part of the whole of our lives, and we all know that what happens outside work affects what we do and don't do at work. This seems especially true for women, because many of us play multiple roles in life simultaneously – at work and at home, in our communities and in our voluntary work.

So it may be important for you to capture these aspects on the Journey Map, bringing into your analysis those key moments from your life outside work and considering how they might have affected the trajectory of your map. Here's how it proved useful for Olivia.

CASE STUDY   Olivia's success at work and crisis outside work

Olivia said that she had never really regarded herself as successful at all, and she wasn't confident about herself or her future. But the first version of her Journey Map reminded her of some important successes which she had achieved. And then she added a second set of key moments from her life *outside* work to her Journey Map. 'It was a rather shocking insight for me,' she said. 'No wonder that I had never really celebrated winning these research grants, or the publication of my first article – they'd always seemed to coincide with something terrible happening outside work, like my grandfather's death or the diagnosis of my mother's illness.' The exercise of drawing her Journey Map forced her to realize that she had actually achieved some success in her field and had simultaneously managed to cope with the tragedies outside work, too. By thinking about what success meant to her, she changed her definition of it so that it covered both her work life and her home life. And she felt more confident about the future when she saw more clearly what she had actually done in the past.

FIGURE 2.6   Olivia's Journey Map

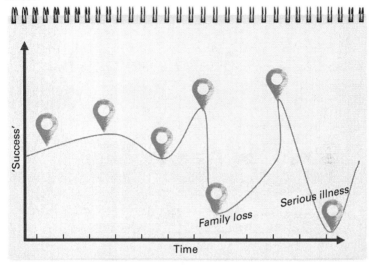

Olivia's Journey Map

Olivia added to her Journey Map some events from her life outside work – including the death of a beloved grandparent and her mother's serious illness.

Step 6: What do the different phases of your working life look like?

At this point, it's easier to make sense of the map if you step back from the detail and think about the different phases of your journey so far. By doing this, you will see more clearly some of the reasons why your journey has developed as it has – and, most of all, you will learn more about the transitions and changes you have made along the way.

FIGURE 2.7 Identify the phases

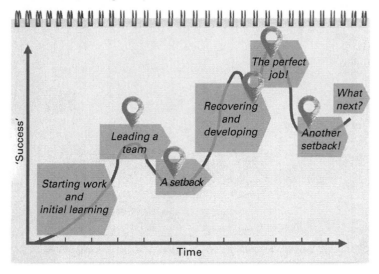

Identify the phases

For example, initial learning, uncertainty, maturing, further development, or whatever seems right to you.

So, as you look at your map, the next step is to define those specific blocks of time around and between key moments. During each of these phases, you will probably have been doing similar sorts of work, and the trajectory of your Journey Map line will also be similar. The phases might be times of learning and rapid progression, or times of stagnation. There might be a phase during which you reached a plateau in your career, and it felt like you were standing still. Or there might be phase in which you experienced turbulence or even a crisis.

Some phases will be obvious and you will see them almost instinctively, while others may be less so. The best answer is almost always the one which first occurs to you. You will be able to describe some of the phases easily, too, in terms of what you did – perhaps a time of searching, or settling in to a new role, maybe a time when your focus was outside work because of what was happening in your private life. So, as you define the phases, give each one a label.

This focus on phases and their timing can generate some useful insights for your future plans, as Alison found when she drew her own Journey Map.

CASE STUDY Timing is everything

Alison is in her early fifties and has had a long and varied corporate career. She found this exercise surprisingly useful in reminding her that strategy is not just about *what* to do, but *when* to do it.

'I quite enjoyed drawing the Journey Map, reflecting on the various jobs I have had over the years in marketing, then business development and finally in HR. It may not look very neat, but it was useful. I hadn't realized that I tend to make a really big change around every seven years or

FIGURE 2.8 Alison's Journey Map

Alison's phases

Alison's map shows the phases of her work and the key events in her life outside work. She has added a future key event, too – the point at which her son will leave home to go to university. Her Journey Map highlights her key question: what shall I do next?

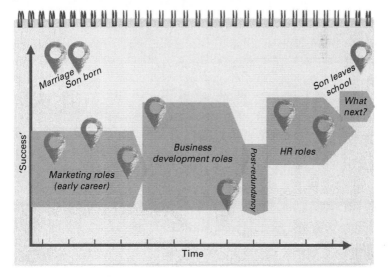

45

so. Obviously there are other times when I've changed jobs, maybe been promoted or moved into the same kind of role in a different company. But the big changes in my working life – where I've moved to a completely different sector, for example – happen around the seven-year point. I really hadn't noticed that before. And when I added to my Journey Map the things that have happened outside work – getting married or having my children – I could see the connection. Things coincided! That might explain why I've been feeling unsettled recently. If the past is any guide to my future, I think I am coming to the end of a phase, and might even be overdue for a change! And my youngest child is just about to leave school, so life outside work will be different. I'm hoping it will open up some new opportunities, as I cope with what my friends call empty-nest syndrome. So I really do need to look again at my strategy.'

Step 7: What generic external events have affected your working life?

So far, the Journey Map concentrates on your individual working life and the specific things that have happened to you. But the external context affects us all to some degree, although this may vary depending on your job, your age or where you live. Most importantly, your context may well determine the number of available options for you as you consider your next step. It's worth looking back to examine the effects of context and of those obvious external events on your working life in the past, so that you understand your story fully.

This step in the exercise is about considering the external, organizational factors which are not specific to you – this is not the same as Step 5, where you looked at events in your life outside your work. Here, you are looking at those events which will have affected many people, such as a period of economic growth or recession. Some factors may be more specific to the industry or sector in which you have worked, such as techno-logical changes which allowed or required you to work differently. Others may be specific to the organization for which you worked, such as a merger or acquisition. Mark these external events on your Journey Map. What was their effect on you? For example, did the external event precipitate a change, or force you into making a transition straightaway?

Step 8: Review: What is this exercise telling you?

Now that you have your first draft Journey Map, sit back and reflect on it – have a cup of tea or coffee, take a breath, and take your time. It's hard to predict what you might learn from this exercise, since everyone's journey looks different. In my experience, though, everyone who has done this exercise has learned *something* from it, gained some insight which they hadn't seen before. Something will leap out at you from your map – but if you need more suggestions, go back to the examples in this chapter of women who have also done this exercise and what they learned from it. And let's return to Abby's story to see exactly how the Journey Map exercise helped her.

CASE STUDY   An insight from looking back

Abby started the Journey Map exercise by simply making a list of each new role she had held within her organization, in chronological order, on the date when she started it. Then she gave herself a score to show how successful she felt she had been in each one – not always immediately successful, though; sometimes it had taken many months to settle in to some of her jobs. When she turned this into a drawing, she could see some interesting patterns: 'I could see again and again the initial euphoria of getting the job and starting it, followed by the end of the honeymoon period when things looked harder than I thought. That was definitely the case when I moved to a completely new part of the business. But gradually, in almost every job, things got better; I realized that it was getting to know people in the team and learning to work effectively with them that was key for me.'

Looking back using the map, Abby recognized that this network of people whom she knew and who trusted her had helped her to get things done. She'd been able to pick up the phone to someone she knew well in another department to ask a question, or persuade someone to join her team for a workshop to develop some alternative approaches to a problem. That was the light-bulb moment: in some ways, she had actually been in a liaison role for years, although that didn't appear in her job description. And there was nothing to suggest that she couldn't do the same thing in a new organization. So, feeling more confident, Abby started to rewrite her CV with this new perspective and downloaded the application form for the new job.

EXTENSION IDEAS

- Do this exercise with a colleague and share the story that the map reveals. Ask each other about the high points and what was so good about them, as well as about the low moments and how you got yourself out of them. Does your story make sense to them when you relay it to an outsider? Are there insights which you may have missed and which they might see because they are hearing the story for the first time?

- Ask yourself the hindsight question about particular events: if this happened to you again, would you do something different? Would you react differently? Would you take action sooner, or plan more carefully?

- When you made a job change, was that because of something in your life outside work (a 'situational determinant') or because of your own choice (a 'personal determinant')?

- When you look at the different phases of your working life, what happens at the intersection of those phases – where one phase moves into the next? Are those times of turbulence which were difficult for you? Or did you relish the new opportunities that opened up? Some women find that, by thinking deeply about their transitions, and maybe even plotting them in more detail, they can almost build themselves a recipe for making changes – a list of what has worked for them in the past that could be useful for the future.

- Does the Journey Map reveal something that isn't currently reflected in your CV but that you should add? For example, the ability to learn rapidly about a new industry from your experience of moving into similar roles but in different sectors? Or about your frequent assignments to lead demanding projects in your area of expertise? If you want to take action immediately, start by reviewing and rewriting your CV in the light of these new insights.

- Does your Journey Map look different if you do the exercise again, but this time with a different definition of 'success'? Sometimes a second attempt with a deliberately different axis on the graph is surprisingly revealing – so if you chose an external definition of success, such as promotions, try the exercise again with a more internal definition – like satisfaction or happiness, for example.

- Sometimes, women like to use this exercise to explore the intersection between their private life and their working life, by drawing two different lines on the same graph – for example, plotting their sense of happiness at work and, separately, in their life outside work. For some women the lines show a remarkable similarity but for others they are interestingly different.

- What external events are likely to affect your working life in the future? Maybe take a moment to think about the external events which might affect your next phase in the same way that external events have affected you in the past. These might be organizational changes which you know are coming, or the big national changes which are already under way. Or they might be planned events, such as retirement dates, or the date on which a contract is scheduled to end, a house move, or the date when your children leave home. Beginning to think about what lies ahead is a useful transition to the second section of this work – focusing on the future.

SUMMARY

- The first stage in building a strategy for your future is to reflect on your past. By mapping out your working life so far, you will see more clearly what you've done and achieved, and what you have learned that you can use in plotting out a new future map.

- Your Journey Map is more than just a CV: it will also show how you felt about what you were doing – how successful you felt you were at each stage, whatever success means to you. By seeing the key moments in your working life and the transitions from one phase to another, you can see the skills and strengths you've developed which will help you in implementing your new strategy.

- When you review what you've done so far, you'll see the key points you want to build into your strategy for the future: roles you liked, organizations you enjoyed working for, as well as the experiences which you don't want to repeat.

What's next?

Now that you have reflected on the past, you might want to reconsider the present: how things are going right now in your working life. The next chapter offers you a way to look at your current situation more objectively.

FIGURE 2.9 Worksheet: Your Journey Map

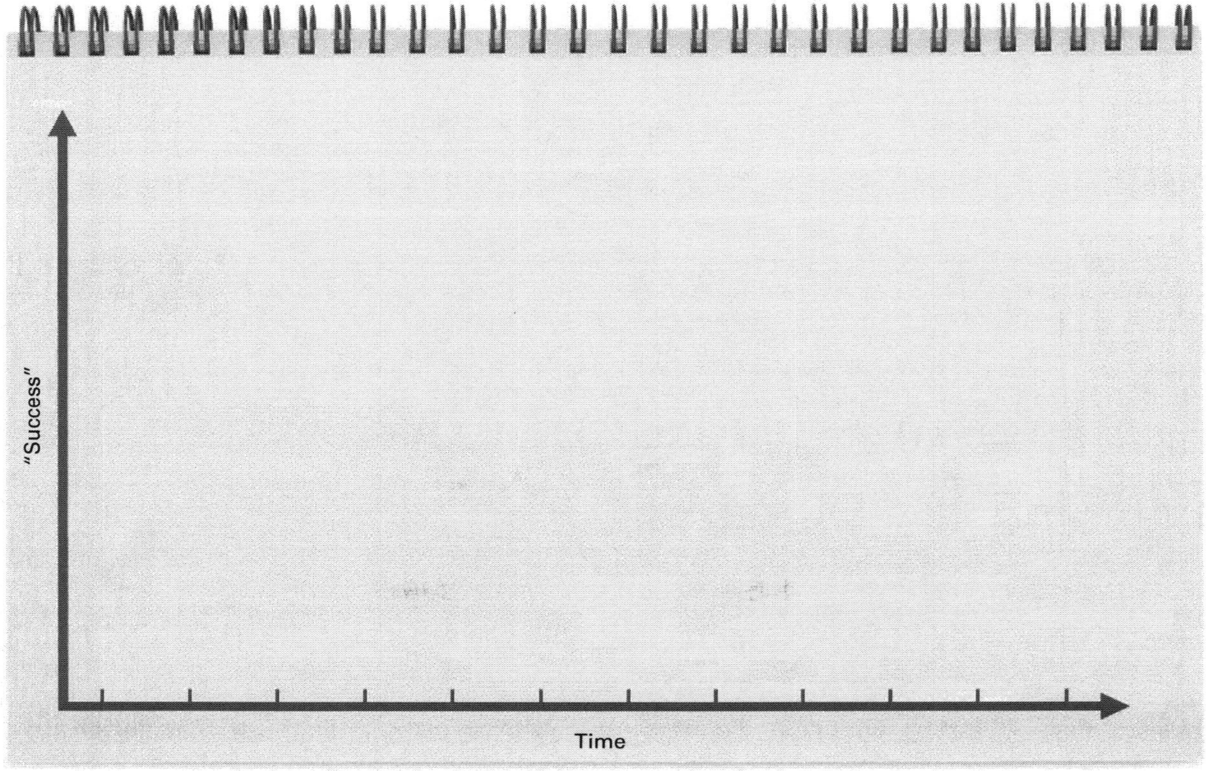

CHAPTER THREE

What is working well right now: your Personal Dashboard

What's working well for you in your working life right now? What are you less happy with? Where are you spending your time, and what's the balance in your life like? Are you spending time on the things which matter most to you?

Why this matters to you

Sometimes there is a nagging sense that things at work are not quite as good as they should be. At other times, you may feel that there definitely has to be a better way of devising a working life than this! Whatever your situation, there's probably a reason that you've picked up this book, which may become clearer with an objective review of your current situation.

There are various ways you might do this. Some women choose to set up a series of sessions with a professional coach to look at the problem. Or even a conversation over coffee with a friend might help. However you choose to do your review, a good place to start is to gather some data about how you actually use your resources. Where are you spending your time, energy and attention? Literally mapping this out can be very revealing.

This data may tell you what's not working, and it will certainly show you what the balance is like between your work life and home life. We normally use the phrase 'work–life balance' when we talk about these issues, but this phrase does have an underlying assumption that your *real* life only happens outside work. And for many of us, that's simply not accurate: work can be an important source of meaning and satisfaction and part of our identities. So in this chapter, we will talk about 'work–home balance' and use that reframing to help you reflect on the balance between what you do at work and everything you do outside work, whether that is at home for the good of the family, or elsewhere for the benefit of your community.

We'll cover some simple questions about resource allocation at the start of the strategy review process for two reasons. First, they are quite easy to answer, whether you choose to do some detailed diary analysis or simply estimate what happens during any working week, so it helps us to get under way. But second, they are useful questions to be able to answer properly. Your answers may suggest to you some immediate actions that you can take now, without any further work, to make your working life more manageable. For example, when I first did this exercise, it became clear to me that I wasn't spending enough time on activities that sustain me – on health and exercise – or on creative activities that stimulate. Despite reading many excellent books on productivity, I wasn't actively planning the allocation of my time, but just allowing things to happen. My 'To Do' list drove my day, rather than me driving my day.

The idea

Gathering some objective data about your life right now will help you to develop a sense of exactly what's happening and why. We'll call this objective picture of the way you spend your time a 'Personal Dashboard', just like the Management Information Dashboards that organizations use. Dashboards draw together data about both activities and progress, and present the data graphically to make it easy to read and understand. Instead of focusing on one aspect, we can see the whole picture. Your Personal Dashboard will help you answer questions such as: are your priorities getting enough attention? Are you also investing in your own well-being sufficiently so that you can keep going? The Dashboard might also help you to generate some simple metrics which you can use in future to keep track of progress and see how things are improving.

Part of the value of this exercise is aggregation, bringing together data which, by itself, may not mean that much. When it's set against other information, it can point the way to some useful changes. Seeing the interrelationships and overlaps of how we spend time and energy helps us to understand the trade-offs we are making, consciously or unconsciously. For example, if you have some tight deadlines on key projects right now, you may be willing to tolerate a dip in your sense of well-being because you know that getting these projects completed will be worth the effort. But if you are not making the progress you want *and* you are putting in the hours, then there may be another issue which you need to address.

So, in this chapter, we'll look at your life at work (and outside to some extent) in four areas:

1 How you spend your time – at work, outside work, on your own development or on caring for others.

2 What your priority projects and tasks are right now and how they are progressing.

3 What really matters to you in your work and life right now – what your key success factors are.

4 Your own well-being – your mood and energy, which are the fuel levels that propel you at work and outside.

Bringing these metrics together, and examining the information objectively in graphical form, should prompt you to manage your resources more consciously – and therefore probably more effectively. As you do this, you may want to add your own elements to your dashboard, or to redesign it – you should feel free to customize it to work for you.

Parallels with corporate strategy

If you were on the board of a business, one of the key issues you would examine regularly would be exactly where the organization's resources are being used. For example, do organizational units have the right budgets? Which projects have the most funding? Organizations know that resource allocation is a critical part of decision making, and so they build operational data into a Management Information Dashboard. This will usually contain a variety of graphical representations, such as pie charts or progress reports, showing what is happening now in the organization; these are pictures of the present. This data is regularly refreshed and reviewed, and it guides the decisions about what to do next.

There is also a focus on reporting on progress in important areas, because one of the key decisions that senior leaders and boards have to make is about prioritization. These are almost always hard decisions because, for them – just as for us as individuals – there is rarely enough resource to do everything. Something has to give, be de-prioritized, and trade-offs have to be made. The trick is to make such decisions consciously rather than simply pretending that you can get everything done. And you have to review those choices regularly, of course.

So, in the corporate world, organizations put considerable effort into data collecting and reporting, because they're critical leadership tasks. The board needs to notice when something is not progressing properly and consciously re-prioritize and reallocate resources to get back on track – and they can't do that without good information.

Once again, this is an idea which we can usefully adapt as part of our own strategizing process. Choosing where to invest our resources – time, energy, attention or money – is one of the key decisions we can make, and most of us don't make those decisions consciously. We may not even think of it as a choice, most of the time. We let the demands of the meeting schedule dictate what we do. We let other people put things on our 'To Do' lists, and therefore effectively they decide how we allocate our time. There's no need to be too hard on ourselves: sometimes we can't avoid this. Often, though, we have more choice than we think we do, and making the allocation of your time a conscious decision can be both effective and liberating. It's also a key aspect of strategy formulation, as we know from the Strategy Triangle.

This exercise starts with a review of how you spend your time now, and, for us, the collection of data can take much less effort than for a large corporate company, as you will see later in this chapter.

The underlying research

The justification for including a review of the present as you develop a strategy for the future is not just because good strategy is built on a realistic assessment of the current situation. There is also a particular significance for women in doing this exercise. Research into the careers of female chief executives undertaken by the University of Oxford indicates that one of the key moments in a successful working life for women is the point at which they take active ownership of their own careers (Athanasopoulou *et al*, 2017). Although the women interviewed have each had different career journeys, the various stories they tell about the journey of their working lives all seem to have this moment of realization and acceptance. The moment when they decide to accept the trade-offs and compromises which have to be made and to manage them consciously.

These key moments are not all the same. Sometimes, women talk about having to take on responsibility as a carer early on in their lives. Sometimes it was a major promotion or having to deal with a crisis of some kind. Whatever the cause, this sense of active ownership and management of their careers seems to stem from these incidents and becomes very significant in the story of their lives. Maybe your Journey Map from Chapter 2 has such a moment in it.

The research presents three underlying dimensions of the idea of ownership. Many women have found these useful in under-standing what 'taking ownership of your career' might mean in practice.

First, there is the idea of *self-acceptance*: acknowledging that your own abilities and energy are what you have to work with. One of the routes to self-acceptance is to sharpen your under-standing of who you are and what you have done in life. This might come through feedback, such as 360-degree reviews at work from colleagues or as part of your performance appraisal. It might come from psychometric profiling to give you a greater understanding of your psychological preferences. But it also comes from self-reflection, the opportunity to consider in a structured way how you got here – we covered this in the previ-ous chapter. When you drew your own Journey Map, you may have realized how far you have come since you started work, and how much you have already achieved or coped with. Whatever you found, the exercise should have clarified your sense of yourself, and therefore of self-acceptance.

The second theme is the idea of *self-development*. Women talk about taking their own responsibility for their development, not simply waiting for the end-of-year performance review to generate ideas for a course they can attend. But there is a balance to be struck here, between accepting yourself, your strengths and limitations, and choosing to develop yourself and your skills. There is more about this in Chapter 7, when we look at the Strengths model.

Third, there is the idea of *self-management*, and that is what this chapter is about. Self-management implies a conscious control of the activities in a working day: not just *what* we do, but *how* we choose to do it. And it implies that if we find ourselves doing things at work which we neither like nor are good at, which don't contribute to the betterment of the world and which may not even be a part of the job we are paid for, then we should manage ourselves more actively. Find a way of doing something different, something more useful, more interesting and, in the long run, more sustainable.

By building your Personal Dashboard, you will be better able to adjust what you do at work, making conscious choices about when, where and how to work. If you don't like what your Personal Dashboard data tells you about your life, you have the opportunity to change it – or at least to tweak it right now and plan for more significant changes later.

CASE STUDY Michaela's decisions

Michaela knew that she had overstretched herself. She didn't feel particularly well and wasn't happy either at home or at work. She really couldn't go on like this. But her job as a lead researcher in the art history department of a major university was frantically busy, and she just couldn't see a solution.

The Personal Dashboard exercise was just what was needed, she said. First, she looked at the allocation of her time over a typical week, and then did the same analysis for a month. The pattern was the same: almost all her waking hours were spent at work, but she had no sense of successful progress to keep her going. Her life outside work mostly consisted of going home to sleep. She was shocked when she saw this vividly represented on a pie chart, but it did at least give her an idea of where to start. She drew herself a target chart: a graph showing how she wanted to spend her time in future, with a better balance during the working week and at least one day at the weekend with no work at all.

Setting this out so clearly forced her to take action. The most obvious thing to change was to stand down from a project group and delegate this role to her new team member, who was keen to take on something significant. But this wasn't enough, so Michaela gave herself an aim: within three months, she wanted to be allocating her time in line with the ideal projection that she set for herself.

Michaela already had a project and task logging system, to keep track of her time, but when she assessed her progress, she could see that, despite the time spent on it, one key project was running well behind schedule. So, a useful focus for the month ahead.

But the most unexpected insight came when she examined her personal key success factors – those overarching aspects of her life which have no particular deadline but with real significance. Michaela realized that most weeks she spent almost no time on anything creative. Yet exercising her creativity was one of the main reasons she had come into this field. So she deliberately reintroduced time into the working week when she could work on her own research and think creatively about her own ideas. To make that work, she had to stop doing something else, or at least renegotiate the deadline; she chose her lowest priority project and made an appointment to see her boss, to discuss delaying the work until the autumn.

The exercise: guidance

These four short exercises will help you to assemble your own Personal Dashboard and answer the following questions:

1 Where do you spend your time, and on what?

2 What are your priority projects and tasks, and how are they progressing?

3 What really matters to you right now? What are your key success factors at work and outside and how do you feel they are going?

4 How are you yourself – how is your sense of well-being?

As we've said above, these four questions are clearly linked: for example, if you are not feeling particularly well, it's not hard to see that progress on some projects might be affected. Equally, if your time chart shows that you are spending all of your time on one or two urgent projects, you might well find that some of your non-work key success factors might be adversely affected.

Gathering the data might take some effort, but it doesn't need to be perfect – and many women report that the effort involved is well worth it for the insight you gain. Below you'll find the guidance for each of the exercises and, at the end, some suggestions for ways to review the whole dashboard and what it might be telling you.

Exercise: Time allocation

This exercise is about your time allocation at the macro-level, across a working week or a month, and across competing priorities: work and home, health, your social life, or learning activities.

You can make this exercise as simple or as detailed as you want: the objective is to have in front of you a picture of where your time is spent right now. There is a range of time-tracking apps available to help you if you want to automate the process. One of the easiest ways of doing this is to use spreadsheet software which will generate a pie chart for you from the data you have entered. Here's an example:

1 Start by identifying the categories you want to use in recording your time. Don't have too many – it makes the exercise harder than it needs to be and too time-consuming in itself. Here's a list of possible categories you might want to choose from:

a. Work;

b. Home;

c. Social life;

d. Health/exercise;

e. Learning/creativity;

f. Travelling/commuting;

g. Thinking time/reflecting/time to yourself.

You may not want to use all the categories so choose the most obvious ones for you, and get started – you can redo the analysis whenever you want to.

2 Set up a way of recording the time: you could keep a detailed time log on a simple spreadsheet, or in your online calendar for every working day. Or you could choose to record the time one day a week for a few weeks. Alternatively, you could simply look back over the last week and create a quick summary of where the time seems to have gone, again using your diary.

3 You'll need to record the maximum available hours for the week or the month which you are looking at, and either subtract from that the hours which you spend asleep, or add that category to your chart.

4 Now turn the data into a pie chart. If you are gathering the data on a spreadsheet, you should be able to do this easily.

5 Finally, the review stage: what does this tell you? Are there some obvious changes you could make now, in your working day, so that this allocation of time works better?

You may not necessarily be looking for an even balance of time across the categories: it depends on your current situation. If you have just started a new job, you will obviously be spending more time at work than on anything else just at the moment, and the

FIGURE 3.1 An example time allocation chart

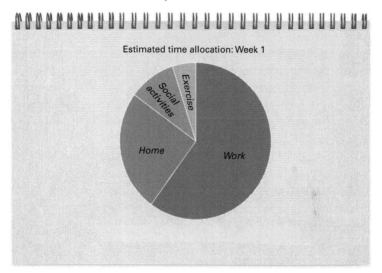

trade-off may well be worth it. But you might want to ask yourself how sustainable this is: how long do you want to continue
with this balance of work and time outside work?

Here's an example to help you get started.

CASE STUDY   Jenny's review

Jenny works in the finance team at her organization, has a baby
daughter, and is also doing a distance-learning MBA to improve her
qualifications. She started this strategizing work because she had two
competing concerns: that she wasn't progressing fast enough in her
career, and because she wasn't satisfied with how well she was doing
outside work. She seemed to be putting in huge amounts of effort and
time and not making the progress she was hoping for.

She began by looking at her calendar and building a simple
spreadsheet to calculate how much time she spent across some specific
categories: at work, with her family, and on her MBA. She gave herself a
fourth category – 'other' – for time she spent commuting, with friends,

and on her health and exercise. She quickly decided that these detailed calculations using a spreadsheet were too much effort, so for one day a week for four weeks she kept a simple time log, recording time spent on those four categories. She then realized that she had to break down the 'other' category into three further categories: commuting (because it was so time-consuming), friends and exercise.

What did she learn? Some of it was exactly what Jenny expected: she had no time at all for friends and exercise most days, since her work took up most of the daylight hours and her family all the rest of the time. But she also found some useful things: she wasn't taking any time at lunch away from her desk, and even 15 minutes of walking could be fitted in most days. She also decided that she could get double value from some of her time if she planned more carefully – for example, meeting a friend at the weekend and going for a walk together. She also realized that she could use the hour a day which she spent driving to work more effectively if she took the train because she could read some of her MBA course material, rather than being stuck behind the wheel in a traffic jam. That was certainly an option.

So in completing this exercise, Jenny began to see some ways of improving her current situation. And by understanding the present more objectively, she developed some insights for her ideal future.

Exercise: Progress on priority projects and tasks

This exercise is a way of asking about the *results* of the time you are spending on your responsibilities at work – the progress on projects and tasks you are working on. Making a simple list of priorities can be very useful, but many people already have their own systems for tracking their work.

This exercise goes a bit deeper, and asks you to assess how well things are progressing. It's a completely honest assessment for your *own* purposes, not to share with anyone else. The idea is to use the simple RAG (Red–Amber–Green) categorization for each of the projects or tasks you are working on. You assess the priority as green if you are satisfied with your progress; as red if you know things are well behind your plan; and amber as a way of alerting yourself to progress which is not yet a problem but might be soon if you don't take any action.

You might choose to add some tasks from outside work, or to make two lists; either way, the idea is to see if the time you are spending really is paying off in terms of progress.

When you look at your diagram, you may decide that the primary reason for a lack of progress is simply that you aren't able to spend enough time on that task. Or you might discover that the project you are spending most of your time on is simply not progressing, so you may have to devise another way of solving that problem, rather than simply trying harder.

This is a dashboard that should help with allocating and prioritizing. Seeing the complete list will help you choose where to focus in the next few days or weeks. As one female leader said to me, 'As long as the plates I am spinning don't actually fall to the ground, I don't have to keep spinning them all at the same

FIGURE 3.2   Progress on priorities

Progress chart

Project/Task	Status	Notes
Office move project		Need meeting with Facilities team
Team recruitment		Behind schedule; get job description agreed
Survey creation		Draft prepared
Personal financial review		Schedule for next month
Book family holiday		Must do this week!
Exercise schedule		Improving

Key: Green   Amber   Red

time. I can take my eye off one or two of them for a few weeks, as long as I come back to them in time.'

Exercise: Your key success factors – at work and outside

This exercise is designed to help you identify what really matters in your life, both right now and in preparing for your ideal future. These are factors that will help you to achieve the success you seek – however you define it – if you can invest time and energy in them. It's just possible that some of these factors might be the same as the projects and tasks you listed in the previous exercise, but this question is really about the underlying or regular things you need to do which will help you. Often, they have no deadline or end date, and that in itself is a clue that you have identified something that is key for your success but that might not appear on any other list.

For example, if you work on your own as a freelancer, it might be vital that you stay up to date with developments in your field, and so you need to attend learning and development events regularly, or go to networking events. It doesn't particularly matter if you do it this month or next month, but you know it's a key success factor for you because it will fuel future work. Or sometimes salespeople say that one of the key success factors is simply how many client calls and meetings they have, because their experience suggests that a proportion of these will turn into actual sales; they may be targeted on sales revenues but they know that simply making the calls and going to the meetings is the underlying critical success factor that keeps them active in the market.

Both of these examples are about activities, but you might want to include some factors which are about outcomes or results: for example, you might want to record your repeat sale rate if you are a freelancer – the number of times a client re-engages you to do some work – as a measure of the quality of your work and your reputation. Sometimes, the factors appear to have very little to do with outcomes but are actually more important than they look. It's sometimes said that if you want to be a successful writer, you must focus on the number of books and articles you *read*. While writing this book, one of my success factors was simply sitting at the keyboard of my computer every single day, even for a few minutes. If I could manage to do that, I would usually find something to write, or to edit.

You might decide to take these success factors from your performance appraisal process at work – the criteria which your employer uses to assess your performance. Or you might decide to bring in some factors which relate to the whole of your life, inside and outside work. The factors you identify may change over time, but the question stays the same: are you making progress on the things that really matter to you right now?

FIGURE 3.3 A hypothetical set of key success factors

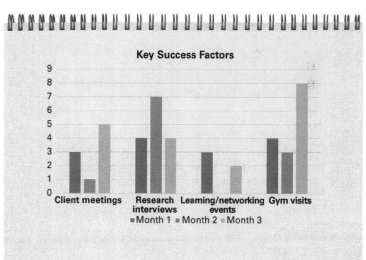

Exercise: Assessing your sense of well-being

This fourth exercise is a simple one, requiring much less detail and less data. It simply asks you to reflect on your energy and mood, the fuel levels that propel you at work and outside. Are things on an even keel for you right now, or at least moving positively? Or is there a downward trend which you might need to address in some way? Some women find it useful to see a pattern which recurs at particular times of the working year, or which is a signal to them that they are approaching burnout.

Use a simple chart like this to plot how well you have felt over the last few months and how well you feel now. The left-hand scale is simply a number from 0 to 100; you can decide for yourself how you might score yourself in a steady state. Then ask yourself what's happening now. Are you in a phase of recovering from a dip? In which case, what are you doing to accelerate your recovery? Or are you on a high at the moment, with plenty of energy to try something new, perhaps?

FIGURE 3.4   An example well-being review

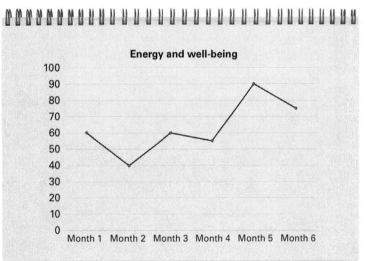

FIGURE 3.5 An example Personal Dashboard

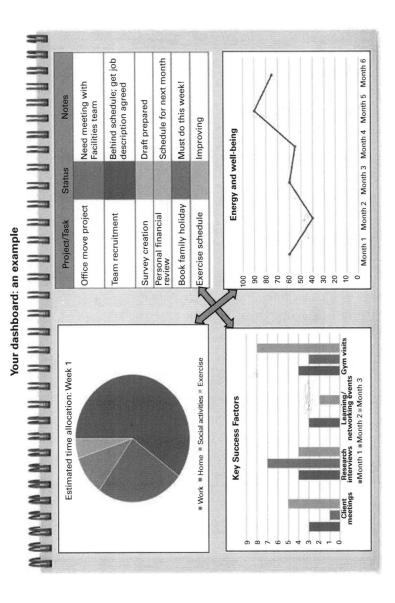

Your dashboard: an example

Project/Task	Status	Notes
Office move project		Need meeting with Facilities team
Team recruitment		Behind schedule; get job description agreed
Survey creation		Draft prepared
Personal financial review		Schedule for next month
Book family holiday		Must do this week!
Exercise schedule		Improving

Estimated time allocation: Week 1

☀ Work ☀ Home ☀ Social activities ☀ Exercise

Energy and well-being

Key Success Factors

Client meetings | Research interviews | Learning/networking events | Gym visits

☀ Month 1 ☀ Month 2 ☀ Month 3

Reviewing your dashboard

Now look at all four individual charts and consider the interplay between them. Sometimes you can see an interaction between them which helps to decide what, if anything, you might want to do to make your working life work better. There are some obvious questions you might ask yourself, depending on what the data is showing you – and here are some to get you started:

- When you look at the time you are spending at work in conjunction with your progress on key projects and tasks, are you happy with the results that you are achieving? Is there some other obstacle which you may need to address?

- Can you renegotiate the deadlines on some projects or tasks, to give yourself more time to do a better job? We often underestimate our ability to do this.

- Could you delegate one of your tasks to a team member who might be glad to have the opportunity to show what they can do? Or is this particular task part of a key success factor for you, which you really don't want to let go of?

- Are you taking enough time outside work? It may not seem like it, but time spent recuperating or doing something different will pay off in terms of your energy and productivity.

- Do you want to schedule some time each week just to think – maybe while getting off the bus early and walking the last part of the journey to work – just some breathing space at the start of the day?

Earlier, you read Jenny's story about the various priorities in her life. Here's what she learned from her dashboard and what she did about it.

CASE STUDY   Jenny's dashboard review

When she took a moment to think about it, Jenny could see that trying to finish her MBA right now was probably too much. She might be able to do it with some better time management, but she wasn't enjoying it at all. She began to see that, in this phase of her life, allocating time for only two priorities – work and family – would be more manageable than trying to do the MBA work as well. And this phase wouldn't last for ever. Once her baby was regularly sleeping through the night, she could restart her course, enjoy it more and be more productive while doing it. So she applied to postpone the final modules of the MBA and deferred her planned graduation by a year. In the short term, she found that she got more done at work and had more energy to contribute to her team. And her line manager commented on this in her mid-year performance appraisal.

When her son was 18 months old, she restarted her MBA work and found things much more manageable: her life was still very busy, but she could just about get everything done. And from time to time she redid the dashboard exercise, to help her keep the right balance between work and home.

EXTENSION IDEAS

Here are some simple ideas to help you get the feel of managing your resources consciously and actively. There are also some implementation tactics which you could decide to start right now:

- Redo the time allocation pie chart for a future week or month, setting out what you would ideally like the allocation to be. You may want to do this by planning where you will spend your time across an ideal week; that will give you a short-term target to help you manage your time better.

- Experiment for a week with planning your day not by task but by time: set a start and end time for your working day and actually leave at that time. You may need to carry over some key tasks to the following day, but this is practice in consciously managing your time, rather than allowing the 'To Do' list to control your day.

- As an experiment, reduce the time of your most regular meetings from an hour to 45 minutes. You can fit more into the day or, even better, give yourself a 15-minute gap at the end of each meeting to do the actions generated out of that meeting and prepare for the next one.

- Try a day of micro-scheduling: planning your day in five-minute blocks, including time for the basic human activities of eating and sleeping. Some people find the attention to such detail tiresome, but some people say that planning ahead in so much detail makes them much more conscious of how they use their time – and even though they may not stick to the plan, they see the benefit.

SUMMARY

- Good strategy reviews begin with an appraisal of the current situation. Creating your own Personal Dashboard will help you to see objectively what's working now and what isn't.

- The dashboard brings together data (eg about where you spend your time), categorization (eg about priority projects and key success factors) and your judgements (eg about your sense of well-being).

- Seeing this objective data will help you with your own self-management and strengthen your sense of ownership of your career.

- The example and the exercise cover four elements of a Personal Dashboard but you should feel free to add other items and customize the tool to work for you.

- Your dashboard may provide insight about *why* something is happening or it may simply serve as an illustration of what's happening in your life right now. Either way, it will be a useful foundation to help you with the next part of your strategy work.

FIGURE 3.6 Worksheet: Your Dashboard

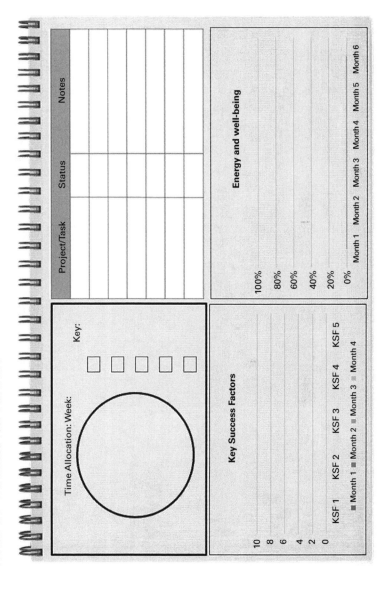

What's next?

If you have done any of the exercises in this chapter, you will now have a clearer sense of what's working in your current situation and what isn't working, what you are satisfied with and what you want to change.

But the question now is: what do you want to change it *to*? What are some of the options for your future?

Envisaging your future

Four different approaches

Stage 2 of this book is focused on your future. This is where we start the hard part of strategy work, designing and defining the 'to be' situation that you are looking for. After the exercises in Stage 1, you'll know more about where you are now. But simply posing the question 'So, what does my ideal future look like?' usually isn't enough. In this second stage, we will look at different ways of answering that question. The exercises in each chapter are designed to give you a range of different perspectives and to make it easier to find an answer that works for you in this phase of your working life.

CHAPTER FOUR

The work that matters most to you: the Ikigai model

When you think about the range of things you do at work, what matters most to you? What kind of work do you see yourself doing as part of your successful working life?

Why this matters to you

Success means different things to different people. Many people say that success at work is about doing something they love and are good at, in an organization which makes a contribution to the world and which rewards them for their effort. It's more than merely 'finding your passion', which is often quoted as the main element of a successful working life. Rather, it's a combination of several factors. There is a particular joy in using your skills to do something you are passionate about but which is also useful in the world. And if you can find a remunerated role doing that work, in an organization you admire, you have all the ingredients for a happy and successful working life.

As you plan ahead, it will help you to know what kinds of work you want to build into your strategy. If you can sharpen your definition of what success means to you at this stage of your life, you'll be better able to draw a map to help you to get there.

The idea

The Ikigai idea explained and used in this chapter will help you to see what you really want to keep in your working life and to suggest what might be missing right now. It's helpful at this stage to examine the end results from the range of things you do at work, both in psychological and economic terms. This model is particularly good for individual strategies because it adds this dimension of outcomes: it asks the question, 'What do I get from my work?' as well as 'What do I give through my work?' This is a different focus from the exercise in Chapter 3, where you assessed the progress and priority of the things that you do; this chapter gets you to think about what these activities bring to you, what they mean to you. It's not just about what you are passionate about, but about three other aspects, too.

Ikigai is a Japanese concept, and there isn't an exact English translation. The word is derived from two Japanese words: *iki*, meaning life, and *kai*, which is sometimes defined as 'realization of hope and expectations'. Although derivations vary, the word '*ikigai*' is often translated as 'your reason for being'. It's not just a single idea but a whole philosophy about the importance of meaning in our lives and about how to live day to day so that our purpose is at the heart of everything we do. Books about this concept cover a whole range of aspects: spiritual discussions, physiological insights and advice about food, as well as about achieving the psychological state of flow in one's activities.

Here, we're using a simple, westernized version of this idea to help think about your working life in relation to your reason for being. Whatever your definition of success may be, if you can use your skills in a job that feels important to you and which allows you to pay the rent, it will be easier to get up in the morning. So, do you have all the ingredients you need for success? Do you know what might be missing? The Ikigai idea in this chapter will help you to examine everything you do and map it across four categories:

- job responsibilities that you can be paid for;
- the tasks you do because you know that your world needs them;
- the activities you undertake because you love doing them;
- those things which you are really good at and do for the joy of using your skills.

By focusing on these four categories, we are once again repurposing a set of ideas to help you to devise your strategy. This simple structure is designed to get you to focus on specific parts of your strategy: the resources you have and the opportunities you might find to do useful remunerated work using those resources. The point of the four categories is that they overlap; some of your job responsibilities are things you love doing, but maybe not all of them. Some of the things you are good at are really important to your world, and some may be less significant but are part of what you are paid for.

This point is often illustrated as a type of Venn diagram, showing the Ikigai categories.

FIGURE 4.1 The Ikigai model

The simplified diagram illustrates the idea that your Ikigai – your reason for being – comes from the overlap between all four categories. Although this book focuses on the strategy for your working life, it's true to say that your Ikigai might be found in your work or in your life outside work, or in a combination of both. That's one of the reasons why this model is so useful for women: it offers the opportunity to explore the significance of the other roles that women play and the other responsibilities we have. The line between work and home can sometimes be blurred and the Ikigai model opens up consideration of the whole of your life as part of your strategy review.

But we'll start with a focus on your working life and an assessment that helps you to see which activities are part of your ideal future. Activities at work which score on all four categories will be key ingredients in your new strategy. They will make you happier and more successful at work, as well as solvent.

The easiest way to see how this might apply to a working life is through an example.

CASE STUDY   Finding the ideal job

Ava always loved numbers, even as a child, and her training as an accountant has given her the chance to develop her skills and to use them. She's worked in finance roles in all sorts of organizations, both large and small, in the private and public sectors. But she also likes working with people, explaining, teaching, and helping them see through the issues they face. This combination of skills and interests propelled her into a senior role in a commercial accounting practice. For a while, this felt like success: she had a job she enjoyed and was good at, and she was well paid.

But gradually she began to feel that there was something missing in her working life. It wasn't quite as satisfying as before. It didn't seem to mean as much to her. So, when her children had grown up and she had fewer financial responsibilities, she decided that this was her moment to make a big change. She took on a finance role working for a charity focusing on mental health provision in the local community. At this stage of her life, she could manage on the smaller salary, which was all they were able to offer. She then discovered that the satisfaction in contributing to the organization's work more than made up for the reduction in salary, just as she had hoped. She was able to use her skills and experience in paid work that she loved, working for an organization which made a visible difference to people in the community.

As this example shows, you might choose to balance the ingredients of your strategy in various ways at different times. Ava was happy with a working life that scored on three of the four categories, given her stage of life. The key thing is to understand what the activities in your working life offer you and the world in terms of satisfaction, joy, money and meaning.

So the model is not just about finding the one single central sweet spot. It has three other uses. First, it's a diagnostic tool that might help you to see exactly what's wrong with your current situation, or what's missing. Second, this diagnosis can help to define some possible solutions. Third, it's a useful way of screening new opportunities to make sure that they really will be as good as they look.

Using Ikigai as a diagnostic tool

The definition of Ikigai implies that you are looking for the activities in your working life which cover all four categories. But if your analysis shows that your work covers only two or three of the categories, as is often the case, there's a clue for your future strategy. You'll be able to see the missing ingredients. There are options here, of course: your work is only part of your life, and you might choose to develop something outside work which compensates for what is missing. Some of the women who have done this exercise have taken precisely that option, as the case studies in this chapter show.

Let's take a simple example. If you have just taken up a completely new role, a paid job which you love, but you are not (yet) particularly good at it, your analysis will look like this:

FIGURE 4.2   A lack of skill

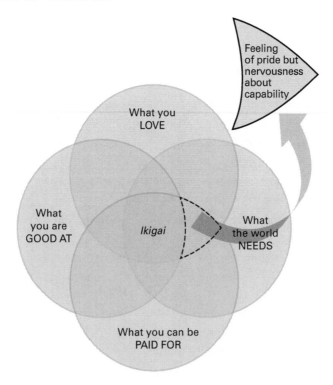

You'll probably have a sense of pride but also nervousness as you build up your skills so that you can do the job well. Once you've done that – with some investment in development, which we will talk more about in Chapter 7 – you might find yourself in the Ikigai sweet spot, which makes all your effort worthwhile.

As a second example: imagine there is something you want to do which you love, which you are good at and know to be vital but which the world won't (currently) pay for. Your Ikigai model will look like this:

FIGURE 4.3   A lack of remuneration

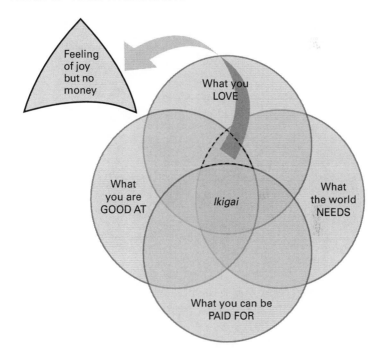

You have some choices here: this activity might have to remain voluntary work or a hobby, or you might have to do some marketing and selling in order to find some funding for it. Some of the strategy options here draw in the other parts of your life to provide the satisfaction, joy or meaning which are part of your definition of success.

Take a third example: where you find yourself missing that sense of making a difference in the world.

FIGURE 4.4   A lack of a sense of contribution

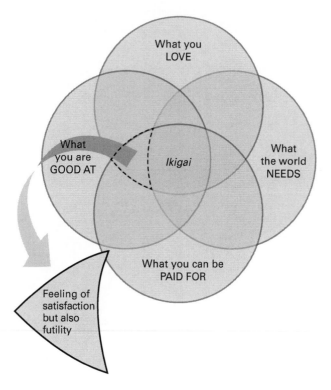

You may have work that you enjoy and are good at, which pays the bills, but which you feel doesn't contribute much to the world. Sometimes, under the pressure of the need to earn a living and support a family, the lack of this aspect is something we might just have to tolerate. Maybe temporarily. But, at other times, in a different phase of life, you might feel that you really have to find this kind of meaning in your professional life. Here's an example of a woman who found herself in exactly that situation.

CASE STUDY   Developing a portfolio

Rachel works in a large professional services firm, loves what she does and is good at it. She is well paid and has been promoted several times. But on bad days, she sometimes feels that her efforts are almost nothing in the face of the world's problems. She would really like to do something, however small, that helps other working families across the world.

One morning, she discovered that her sister had found of a way of doing just this: she had been researching the idea of online micro-lending. Such loans make an immediate and direct difference to individuals in poorer parts of the world who would otherwise have no access to funding. She and her sister started to imagine how much they might be able to help if they had a continuous stream of income to apply to this form of lending. The idea was very appealing. Within two weeks, they had set up a website and created an online business to provide just such an income stream. This business grew out of Rachel's interest in vintage jewellery and her ability to network. While she was posted abroad, she used her free weekends to explore the antique markets in each city and to learn. 'I asked the shopkeepers questions, to learn about values, materials, designs, and they became my friends and my coaches,' she says. Income from their web-based business is split between buying new stock and providing loans through an online micro-lending organization. Over the last five years, they have made loans to women in around 48 countries, making a real difference to them and their lives.

Rachel's portfolio of work – her professional salaried role, her web-based retail business and her lending role – makes up her Ikigai. Collectively, it fulfils her desire to do work which she is good at, which she loves, which is needed and which generates income both for her own family and for the micro-lending service.

Using an Ikigai diagnosis to identify possible solutions

Your diagnosis using this model will help you to see some possible solutions. If you now know what's missing from your working life, you might consider the following options:

- changing your job – searching for something that looks more like your Ikigai;

- investing in your own development so that you become good at what you do;
- taking on some additional activity or job which provides that missing element and building a portfolio of work which, taken together, meets all your various needs;
- job crafting – making some minor changes in your existing job so that it becomes more satisfying or you can use more of your skills;
- making some space in your life for a hobby or pastime to provide the fulfilment that is missing from your work.

The approach you choose may depend on your particular circumstances and where you are in your life right now. Sometimes, the right option is a blend of these different solutions. And there are often constraints: it may be hard to persuade employers to invest in development, or the idea of taking on some other activity might seem impossible given how hard you work already. Identifying the obstacles is a key part of strategic thinking, as is defining possible ways around them. Don't be discouraged: many women working on their strategies have been surprised to find that they have more ability to overcome these barriers than they thought they did, because they use the strategy process to devise creative and workable solutions.

The portfolio approach is an obvious way to achieve a sense of Ikigai, as Rachel found: consider taking on more than one 'job' or set of activities if the one perfect job that meets all your needs doesn't exist. It might appear to require more time and energy than is possible at certain stages of life, but, at other times, it can be a very workable answer. One of the other benefits of this multistrand approach is that it provides some insurance, because if you have more than one role, it's most unlikely that you would lose them all at the same time.

And this portfolio option is not necessarily just about paid work, although the demands of supporting a family will sometimes require that. Here's an example of a woman who took this portfolio approach, but by looking outside her work.

CASE STUDY   Finding an interest outside work

A career in human resources had been the obvious choice for Rebecca. Her mother had worked in what was then called personnel management and had always talked about the opportunities to make things better for working people. And it had been a good choice for Rebecca: over her 15-year career, she had worked in various parts of the department, including pay and benefits, employee relations, and as the HR manager. She'd become a Fellow of the Chartered Institute of Personnel and Development and had invested time and energy in her continuing professional development. Her most recent promotion had given her responsibility for developing the strategic HR plan for the whole organization, covering all the different HR functions. She had been delighted to get this job and knew the work was important. After all, this was about developing the business and planning for its future. With this job, she felt she had a real opportunity to help create a kind of working environment in which employees could flourish.

But after three years, she found that she no longer loved the work. The job was now well within her capabilities and felt not so much comfortable as stale. She still spoke of her work with some pride because she had real evidence that her contribution made a difference, but it didn't bring her any challenge. Some mornings, she felt almost bored.

She knew that she needed to do something. But what? This was her profession, after all. She didn't want to apply for essentially the same role in a different company, and she didn't want to move location because that would disrupt her family. She could see various possible next steps, but none of them felt obviously right. She even considered stepping back to a more junior managerial role in an operational department, so that she could focus more on implementation and less on planning.

While she thought about her options, she started to devote some time to one of her main hobbies, something she loved – tai chi. She began to train as an instructor and found it fascinating and absorbing. And she noticed a couple of immediate benefits. 'I found myself coming back into work with a new spring in my step, feeling more energized, even though I had spent the weekend learning to teach small children the basics of tai chi, which is not that easy! And secondly, I felt that professionally I had undervalued the importance of learning and development for people. So the way I did my job started to change, as a result of spending time doing something completely different outside

87

work.' Rebecca commented that she found it ironic that for someone who had invested so much in her professional development, it was time spent on a hobby outside work that had revitalized and re-energized her.

But taking on something else, paid or unpaid, at work or outside, is not the only possible solution. In the following example, Moira found that she could make some immediate improvements with a couple of relatively simple changes in her existing job, crafting it to be more satisfying.

CASE STUDY Job crafting

Moira led a small team that worked on the front-line customer service desk, helping people by phone with specific technical issues about their savings plans. 'You might think it's just a call-centre role, but the services which the team provide can be critical in safeguarding people's future financial position,' she commented. She'd been part of the team for three years and had been promoted to the team manager role relatively recently. She liked working with her colleagues and knew that they did a good job. But she really missed the chance to talk to customers herself and found the managerial responsibilities quite demanding. She'd been glad to get the promotion, but didn't feel as much satisfaction in being the team leader as she'd expected.

Using the Ikigai model, Moira saw her situation more clearly. Her role did make a difference in the world, to those customers who called with questions, and she could certainly do the work she was paid for. But she didn't feel that she was in any way an expert, or even getting better at the job of being a manager. And she didn't love it. She realized that her working day didn't allow her any time to do what she really liked to do: finding out about the customer's issue and developing a solution with them.

So, she decided to make two immediate small changes. First, she reorganized her diary so that she could take one afternoon a week to serve on the phone bank herself. This gave her some customer contact that she enjoyed and helped her to keep up to date with the situations that her team faced with customers. Second, she signed up for an introductory management course, to help her understand the team leader role and do it more effectively.

This idea of job crafting is more realistic than it might seem. Most of us have some discretion in what we choose to do at work each day, and when. We might well be able to negotiate the opportunity for a temporary change in some aspect of the job. It may take some planning and some discussion, but it is worth looking for room to do this as part of your strategy implementation. It might be a temporary solution to a problem at a particular phase of your life, or it might be an interim step, to help you get the experience you might need to make a more permanent change.

Finally, there is one other possible solution to consider. It's the one strategic option that always exists: do nothing. Do you really need to find the perfect role at this stage in your working life, right now? You might decide to tolerate the current situation temporarily because this is not the right time to make a big change. If you have caring responsibilities, or are coming back into work after a break, it might be sufficient to find something that offers a salary and that you know you can do. You might decide that you don't need to love the work at this stage; you just need to be able to do it. But somewhere in the future, you may well want some work that really does make it easy to get up in the morning, and that's where the model will help.

The point is that what you need from your working life changes over time. Your Ikigai diagram will look different depending on where you are on your journey, as will the opportunities you choose to explore.

Using Ikigai in selecting the right opportunity

You can also use the four categories in the model as a set of criteria to screen new opportunities. If your current job scores on three categories but is no longer something you enjoy, your feelings of boredom might prompt you to find a new role. In that situation, your version of the model might look like this:

FIGURE 4.5 A lack of interest

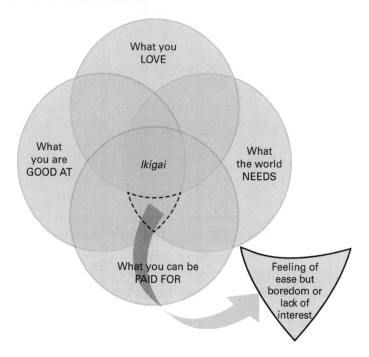

In these situations, it's tempting to take almost any new job just to relieve the tedium of the current role. But use these four categories to review the opportunity before you accept. Do you have the skills to do this job – or could you develop them? Is it a job that you could love? Does it make a contribution to your world? Can you still pay the rent with this salary? You might not find the ideal opportunity which scores on all four categories, but, if not, at least you will know what you are getting and what you might still be missing from your life.

Parallels with corporate strategy

Corporate strategists spend time understanding the organization's core capabilities (those things that it is really good at) as well as the market opportunities to exploit those capabilities. They also understand the distinction between what the world or the market might need and whether anyone will actually pay for it. Organizations that can find the sweet spot between their capabilities and their ability to monetize market needs are usually successful. And their staff are central to this; successful organizations have motivated and skilled staff who love what they do and are good at it.

The Ikigai model draws together the internal dimension of strategy (resources, skills and motivations) as well as the external dimensions (what the world needs and will pay for). In that sense, it's like the Strategy Triangle, which we introduced in Chapter 1. You might not find the Ikigai diagram itself in corporate strategic plans, but you will find consideration of the elements of this model in strategy processes. It is only relatively recently, though, that the idea of overtly examining what the world needs has featured in corporate strategy, with the rise of the corporate social responsibility agenda and environmental, social and governance considerations.

Like the Strategy Triangle, these categories are used in screening and selecting opportunities. In deciding whether to pursue a particular strategic option, the organization will ask itself: can we do this – do we have the skills? Are we motivated to do this – or, as the model puts it, do we love it? Is there a market for it – or, to be specific, is there a customer who will pay for this? And increasingly now, the fourth category is used: does the world need this? Does this make some contribution to the community or at least do no harm?

The underlying research

In Chapter 3, you read about the three themes which emerged from interviews with successful women talking about their working lives: the ideas of self-acceptance, self-development and self-management. The dashboard which you developed was designed to support you with your self-management, but it has a largely internal focus on you yourself, your time and where you are spending it right now.

The Ikigai model helps you to broaden out from that internal focus on the present. You'll add the external dimension to your strategy thinking because your Ikigai map covers both what you do and the skills you have, as well as the opportunities for paid work which the world needs. And the exercise will give you some ideas about the future – what you might do about what's missing from your working life. This might involve some changes in your life outside work, as you saw in the examples. As a result of all this, your self-management will be based on a realistic assessment of what a more successful future might look like for you.

This idea of agency, of your sense of control over your life, is an important constituent in the Ikigai approach (Hasegawa, 2019). Research studies in Japan define the constituent elements of the truly Japanese concept of Ikigai as factors that relate to past experience, present situation and future plans. The point is that the individual's Ikigai may be a function of any one of these factors or of a combination of them. The research also suggests that the sense of fulfilment and control that derives from an individual's Ikigai correlates strongly with health, intellectual activity and social connectivity. And there is a subtle but important nuance in the meaning of the word in Japanese: Ikigai helps you to look forward to your future, whatever your present may be like.

Although we have been using a simplified, westernized version of this idea, there is an obvious parallel here with ideas in this book: of self-management, and of making your own map, drawing from what you have done and are doing now, to make your own way forward.

The exercise: guidance

Since this is an exercise about categorization, we will use a simple table structure rather than the depiction of overlapping circles, but the result will be the same. We'll do this exercise in two phases: first, looking at what you currently do, and then going on to add activities that you would like to build into your future working life.

Step 1

Begin by writing down what specifically you are paid for in your job now; this may be your job description or set out in your annual objectives. For a sales person, it could be a revenue-related target of some kind. Or it might be a generic task such as leading the team, or delivering some new development. If your job description isn't clear enough, do as you did in Chapter 2: take a look at your diary for the last few weeks to consider what you actually do at work.

Step 2

Take this list of activities which you are paid to do and assess each one against the four categories, using a table.

FIGURE 4.6 Ikigai analysis

Activity/Task	Paid for?	Good at?	Love?	World needs?

Start with the activities that you are good at: you should know these from your performance appraisals and feedback. Record your assessment in the appropriate column.

Step 3

Consider which of these activities you love – which parts of your job really bring you satisfaction. Add your assessment to the table.

Step 4

Finally, a rather harder question: which of these activities actually makes a difference in your world – to your team, your colleagues, the organization or, most of all, your customers or stakeholders? The easiest way to get at this is to consider what would happen if you stopped doing one of these tasks. Would this become a problem to those around you? If so, the answer is that the world, or at least the world around you, probably does need this.

Step 5

Take a moment to review your conclusions. Notice if there are parts of your job which score on all four categories, and which are therefore part of your Ikigai. Alternatively, are there some activities which you are paid for but don't like, are not particularly good at, and they don't make a difference to the world? These are useful insights: you'll probably want to do more of the first set and much less of the second set in future.

Step 6

Turn your attention to the future, to the ideal kind of role that you might like, made up of other activities which you'd prefer to do in your future working life. Maybe there are tasks you used

THE WORK THAT MATTERS MOST TO YOU

to do in a previous job which you really relished. Perhaps you have unfulfilled ambitions to do particular things. Add them to the list in the left-hand column.

Step 7

Ask yourself the following questions about this additional list: do you have the skills you need to be able to do this kind of work? Could you find an organization that might pay you for this? And do you feel that the world, or some part of it, might need you to do this?

At this early stage, this might be a messy and idealistic list, but it's useful in beginning to make your map. Here's an example of just this point.

CASE STUDY   Seeing a different direction

'I'm a project manager in the IT function of a government department, and, to be honest, I can't decide whether I like my job or not. You'd think that after four years in the role, I would know, wouldn't you?' Zoe found that doing this exercise helped her to articulate her vague feelings of dissatisfaction and to see what she could do about them, too.

When she listed her activities, she started in the obvious place, setting out the main tasks which appear in her job description. But she added to the list a number of tasks which she spends time on but which aren't formally part of her job. When she'd completed the exercise, her analysis looked like this:

FIGURE 4.7   Zoe's Ikigai analysis

Activity/Task	Paid for?	Good at?	Love?	World needs?
Delivering tested systems on time and on budget	X			X
Project planning	X	X	X	
System testing	X			
Analysis	X	X	X	
Keeping records	X	X		
Solving really difficult problems	X	X	X	X
Organizing people	X	X		X
Presenting plans and progress to management	X	X		

Zoe could see that too much of her job involved tasks that she was good at but did not enjoy (for example, organizing people). She also felt that she'd like to do more activities which used her skills in project planning. And the work that she most enjoyed was solving difficult problems – she would gladly do more of that. This exercise and these insights suggested to her that her career map might lead her in the direction of specialist design and analysis roles rather than project management. She recognized that this might limit her opportunities for progression at work, because her employer tended to promote those who could lead large teams of people. But, on reflection, she thought she might be prepared to make that compromise and her thinking about her next step and career direction was much clearer.

EXTENSION IDEAS

Although this chapter is mostly about defining activities which you want to do more of in the future and build into your strategy, there are some short-term actions you might choose to take, now, even before we finish the strategy thinking:

- Sign up for a development programme: if you have paid work which you love and which is important to your world, but you don't have all the skills you need, read Chapter 7 and explore the options for your development.

- Do market research: maybe you have a set of skills which could be put to better use. If you are good at your job and love what you do, but your current paid role has too small a scope for you or doesn't appear to be meaningful in contributing to the world, do some research about other roles in other sectors or organizations, either full-time or as a voluntary part-time role.

- Network to access job openings: if there is work that you would love to do, that you could be good at and which you know the world needs, but you can't find a paid role like this, use your network to help you. Look for people who do something resembling your ideal job, or who work in organizations which provide similar offerings. Ask if you can talk to them, or even shadow them. There may be more opportunities than you think, or job openings that are similar and cover most of what you're looking for.

- Make a short-term change: if your current role is not challenging or stimulating enough, you could make a short-term change while you search for the ideal job. Take on a voluntary project at work, step up to a temporary role, or reschedule your working week to allow time for the activities which motivate you.

SUMMARY

- Building a working life which gives you satisfaction, joy, a sense of contribution and remuneration is one definition of success. This definition includes both the internal dimension of strategy (resources – the things you are good at and love to do) and the external (opportunities to be paid and to make a difference in the world).

- The idea of Ikigai is also about your 'reason for being'. The model used here is a simplified concept taken from a broader philosophy – it's repurposed to help you begin to define your strategy.

- The Ikigai exercise asks you to assess your work activities against four categories to identify which mean most to you. These are: things you love to do, that you are good at, which make some contribution to the world around you, and which you can be paid for.

- You could add to this assessment the things which you would like to do in future or have done in the past that you found rewarding and enjoyable. You might also consider your life outside work, since your Ikigai could be found in what you do at work, or outside, or in a combination of both.

- Any activities which score in all four categories – your Ikigai – could form a key part of your strategy work and be reflected in the purpose statement which you will generate for yourself in the next chapter.
- Activities which score on only one, two or three categories could be things you decide to address or drop or tolerate (because they are part of your route to a future role which you really want, or because your life outside work is sufficient compensation).
- The Ikigai model will help you to see possible next steps and is also a way of screening new opportunities to see if they are worth pursuing.

What's next?

If you've done the exercise in this chapter, you may now be clearer about what you want to include in your map of your future. If you have found your Ikigai – those activities which are central to your work and which are rewarding psychologically and economically – you'll want to make those the focus of your strategy work. And that's what the next chapter is about: developing a focus through a statement of your purpose.

FIGURE 4.8   Ikigai Worksheet

Activity/Task	Paid for?	Good at?	Love?	World needs?

CHAPTER FIVE

The purpose you serve: the story of you

How would you sum up your 'reason for being' from the exercise in the previous chapter? Why do you do what you do – what's your purpose in life?

Why this matters to you

If you can articulate your sense of your purpose, it will serve you well. It will be a focus for mapping your future, and a touch-stone to help you decide what to do and, just as importantly, what not to do. Being clear about your purpose makes it easier to see your future direction and your next steps.

This is particularly relevant for women, who so often play multiple roles in life, at work and at home. Those roles bring with them a wide range of responsibilities and commitments – sometimes with more to get done than is actually possible. So women frequently have to prioritize, choosing what to do and what to say no to. Of course, that's true for men, too, but sometimes the choices women make are more constrained because we tend to have a wider range of stakeholders whose needs we have to accommodate. For example, a woman with small children whose partner's work requires the family to relocate suddenly has much to decide and even more to do. None of that will be easy, but having a clear statement of purpose will help her revise her plans and make a new map to fit her new circumstances.

There's one key thing to remember: your purpose is not necessarily fixed for the whole of your life. It may well change as you move into a new phase. That might be a slight shift in direction, or a major change as you reach a turning point in life. You'll probably know when that happens because a new opportunity comes along which doesn't fit with your current purpose and isn't part of your plan, but you are still keen to take it up. Maybe it's a secondment offer, or an assignment which is way outside your current experience but that signals a possible change of course. At that point, you might want to look again at your purpose statement. That's one of the reasons for this chapter, so you can redo this exercise whenever you feel you need to.

The idea

Purpose is the animating, organizing and deciding principle for each of us. It isn't about a job title or the targets we are measured on at work. Our purpose has to be something more than 'to have a successful career' or 'to get promoted'. It's not about the meaning of life, but rather a question about the meaning of *your particular* life. And like many important strategic questions, it's both important – vital, even – and hard to answer.

But it's not impossible. This chapter offers you one technique to uncover your own sense of purpose. I use the word 'uncover' rather than words like define, design or generate, because the sense of purpose is usually there in your life, even if you can't describe it. An outsider might possibly see it in the choices you make, in what you say yes to and the opportunities you decline. So the task is often to make this explicit, which allows you to make more conscious and better choices at work and outside.

There are many different perspectives on the idea of purpose, as you can see if you look for books to help you to articulate yours. Some approach this from a religious perspective and are about finding your calling in the sacred sense. Others cover the subject from a therapeutic perspective, using cognitive-based therapy techniques in the search, and are often bound up with the search for happiness. Some books with 'purpose' in the title are really about meditation as a practice. And there are overtly philosophical books about other belief systems, as well as those which apparently take a humorous approach to the whole idea, with a series of quirky questions for you to answer.

You may have been asked to write a statement of purpose before, in an application for a university place or for a job or grant. Often, that's really an expanded CV, simply listing what you have done and what you want to do. But the most important element of a statement of purpose is *why*. Why do you do what you do? You may think you can't answer this question, but you unconsciously answer it every day in what you say yes to and what you refuse to get involved with. When you are doing something that aligns with your sense of purpose, you can feel it; psychologists call it 'flow', and it's characterized by a deep absorption in something that feels both important and enjoyable.

The idea here is to use a storytelling technique to unlock those hidden ideas, to trick the mind, if you like, into revealing some key aspects of your purpose. The exercise relies on the brain's ability to turn ideas into a story with the who, what, how and when, and, in particular, the why. You'll also use your ability to tell the story differently depending on the audience, to see what comes out of the multiple versions of your story. If that sounds daunting, don't worry; the exercise deliberately asks you to work very quickly so that the conscious mind can't filter what comes out in your stories.

Parallels with corporate strategy

In January 2020, the UK's Financial Reporting Council (FRC) published its review of the corporate governance codes in the UK and was explicit about the use of purpose statements in organizations. The FRC clearly regards such statements as significant and distinct from ideas about vision and mission, but they also noted that many purpose statements read more like marketing straplines. Their view is that the most useful statements of purpose reveal *why* the organization undertakes its activity and *why* those activities create value.

The idea has moved into the mainstream of business dialogue, with some organizations now making visible commitment to statements of purpose which link their own activities to a larger social, economic or environmental goal. The reality is that the idea of purpose in organizations is a loosely defined concept at the moment, which embraces both the strategy and the culture of an organization. It encompasses what leaders say about their businesses and what appears in the corporate plan and annual report. There doesn't appear to be a single agreed definition of what purpose is, but almost everyone acknowledges that it should be an organizing principle.

Why do organizations think purpose is important? All leaders know that their focus drives their plans, can inspire their people and might also prevent unintended diversification. People inside the organization certainly know when there is misalignment, when what actually happens contradicts the statements in the annual report or those that are framed on the wall. There has been so much work in so many organizations of all kinds on visions and missions, describing future goals and where the organization wants to get to. This new focus on purpose has a wider scope and a sharper focus on the problem to be solved.

A purpose statement as an organizing principle

Purpose statements should be central to organizations and to individuals as motivators, deciders and organizers. They capture the reasons why people come to work in the morning and deploy their energy on the business of the day. They help people to make hard choices between options – for example, 'this option is closer to our central purpose than that one'.

To be effective, a statement of purpose for an organization needs to contain several elements. First, there is something about the scope of the statement – geographical scope, as well as product or service scope – and then references to the customers or end users who are served by the organization. There may also be a reference to the problems that the organization is trying to solve. Finally, there is also a temporal aspect to this purpose statement: it may change over time. Obviously, it may change if a specific purpose is accomplished – to launch a new organization with new services, for example. There may be a purpose for the first phase of a business, which then flowers into a new and larger purpose. You can see this in the development of many organizations over time, as they go through the kind of journey which we explored in Chapter 2. Avon is one such company, and its history shows a shift in purpose which has also generated changes in organizational structure and focus.

An example: the development of purpose over time

Avon sells cosmetic and pharmaceutical products through local representatives, who effectively run their own businesses; their income comes from the differential between the wholesale and retail price of each product. This provides an opportunity for women to earn money and set up a business in parts of the world where this would otherwise be difficult. But it wasn't always structured in this way; the company was first established in 1886 by a door-to-door salesman called David H McConnell, who actually sold books but used perfume offerings as an enticement to buy. Finding that the perfume was often more interesting to the customer than the books, he then founded the California Perfume Company to develop and sell perfume in North America. It changed its name to Avon Products Inc. in 1939, and during the Second World War turned its manufacturing facilities over to military support. But by the late 1990s, Avon focused on and celebrated the work of more than 2.5 million representatives selling products to more than 650 million customers across 135 countries. In 2005, the company described itself less in terms of its products and more about its customers and representatives: 'The Company For Women' (www.avon.uk.com). Its purpose and focus had moved from selling products to creating small business owners who earn money for their families and communities. As their website says: 'this is the company that puts mascara on lashes and food on tables'. They describe themselves as the 'best beauty group FOR the world'.

With the development of online direct selling, their context has changed considerably. So, their new 'Open Up Avon' strategy includes the idea of rebooting direct selling in the age of the online retailer, as well as 'unlocking digital and e-commerce capabilities'. As a result, their purpose statement now looks more complex and has an even broader scope: 'The Digital Social Selling Beauty Company: the company for women: changing lives of beauty entrepreneurs and democratizing beauty for consumers'.

The underlying research

There are two kinds of research underlying the ideas in this chapter: first, how this relates to the Strategy Triangle; and second, some insights about narrative as a way to elicit and convey meaning.

Purpose and the Strategy Triangle

Purpose is the topmost point of the Strategy Triangle. It's a statement of direction, about the future you are trying to create. Once it's clear, the logical implications fall into place: about how resources are organized and opportunities selected – these are the other two points of the triangle. That's the reason it's worth spending some time on this articulation of purpose: because it should shape your map and your strategy, just as it does for organizations. If it's clear enough, the consequences for what you actually choose to do will be obvious.

Using narrative as a way to elicit and convey meaning

Everyone knows that a story is more interesting to listen to than someone reciting a list. Neurological research shows that a story lingers longer in the brain and is more memorable, perhaps because more of the brain is involved in either telling or hearing it. So a story about your reason for being will be richer and fuller than the list of elements from your Ikigai analysis in the previous chapter. It will mean more – both to a listener and to you (Mead, 2014). Through the story you tell yourself, your purpose will become clearer to you and more accessible as an anchor in your decision making.

What do we mean by a story? It's something which has a start, a middle and an end. It has a chain of connections, of cause and effect, which helps the brain to do what it likes to do:

namely, to make patterns and see connections with our experience. When you take your analysis of what you do that's important to you and the world and create a story from it, you'll begin to unpack some ideas that you may not be quite conscious of. And that will help you to uncover a purpose statement which you can use.

To give you an example of how this might work, here's how Rhiannon used this exercise to develop a new statement of her purpose.

CASE STUDY A change in direction

'Earlier in my working life, I really knew what my purpose was – it just seemed obvious. I was working as an administrative officer in a further education college, helping young people to get through their courses successfully and graduate with qualifications which they could use in the world. As part of my role, I had to do some teaching sessions with new students, telling them about the resources of the college and the best way to make use of them. I liked that part of the work, and it made me a better faculty administrator, too, because I could see things from the students' perspective. And I started to rewrite the online guidance material, because the students asked me some questions which it didn't answer. It was fun working with these young people – and if you'd asked me at that stage of my life what my purpose was I'd have said something like: '*I serve the purpose of helping our students navigate their course successfully to go into the world with qualifications they can use.*'

But no job stays fun for ever, and after a good few years I started to feel a bit of an itch to do something different. I remember the moment when I could see what that might be – it was at the end of a review meeting, looking at all the preparations for this year's intake of new students, when a colleague said to me – partly as a joke, I think – 'You could write the book for new students entering FE colleges, you know!' I was very struck by that, and I thought I should follow up on the idea. I drafted the outline of a few chapters and went to the Faculty Dean to talk about a proposal for the college to publish it. They liked the idea, amazingly. So, suddenly I actually had to do it! Instead of focusing on registered students at my college, I'd be writing for applicants, school leavers in the months before they even applied. I wanted to make sure that I understood what they might need to read in the book, so I thought I ought to volunteer to do more marketing and outreach work in schools. My working life seemed to be undergoing a big change – I literally did different things during my working day. I wanted a clear statement to help focus all these new activities, and so I spent some time trying to set out my new purpose in words, as simply as I could. I used the multiple-story technique to help clarify my thinking, and eventually I came up with this: '*I serve the purpose of encouraging school students to understand what college could offer them and to make wise choices about whether and where to go to college, so that they can prosper in life.*' That was a good enough way of describing my new focus as an anchor for my new strategy.

Rhiannon makes a useful point about what you are aiming for as you do this exercise: a 'good enough' description will be just that – good enough to use as you formulate your strategy. It doesn't have to be perfect, and the exercise should be enjoyable as you develop your statement. And as you work with your draft statement using the exercises in later chapters, you might find yourself making some small changes to it to make it feel more realistic. Many people find that they want to do that – you'll see some examples in Chapter 6.

The exercise: guidance

The objective of the exercise is to generate three very short stories which describe what you do and what problem you are trying to solve in your working life – and to write them very rapidly. This is a way of accessing your subconscious ideas, rather than thinking slowly and carefully about how to write a purpose statement. Your stories will focus on your working life but might also have elements of your private life – because, of course, your work is a part of your life. Don't worry too much about the scope of the story, but tell the story of what you do, whether that's paid or unpaid, or both. Here's the guidance for the exercise.

Step 1

Deliberately working quickly, write three different versions of a very short story about what you do, when, where, and why you do it.

Imagine telling the story to three different people of different ages, genders and backgrounds. For example, to your grandmother, to the 10-year-old boy next door and to someone you have just met, who doesn't know you at all. Be as specific as you can in visualizing who you are telling the story to.

You might want to draw on the insights from the Ikigai exercise as you do this.

Step 2

Scan all three versions of your story: look for common themes, words, ideas or parts of the story that appeal to you strongly, which seem to be absolutely accurate or feel right. Take a coloured pen and circle those parts of the story that appeal to you.

Step 3

Using those words and phrases, develop a fourth version of the story, making it as short as possible.

Step 4

Translate the key phrases from this fourth story into a working version of your purpose statement, in the following format: 'I serve the purpose of...'

You may not be entirely happy with your rough-draft purpose statement, but continue to use it as a working version, particularly when you go into the exercise in the next chapter. Over time, you may find that you gradually start to modify your statement, developing something that is clearer or feels bolder. But, at this point, the test is simply whether it feels broadly right, and sufficiently clear that you can work with it in the rest of this book, maybe tweaking it as you go.

You can do this exercise in any format – the words are more important than the layout. But to help you, as always, there is a simple worksheet at the end of this chapter, mostly designed to encourage you to write three different versions and to make each one as concise as possible. There's also some space to generate a fourth version, using the most appealing parts of the other three versions.

And here is one more example to help you: the set of stories that Rhiannon wrote as she was developing her new statement of purpose.

CASE STUDY   Rhiannon's purpose stories

Story 1: As told to her grandmother

I've been working with registered students who are already at college, but now I want to work with younger school students who are deciding whether to go to college at all. I can help them decide if it's for them, and what kind of course and location might suit them, because I've seen so many students over the years. Obviously, I can't talk to them all individually so I need to offer advice and help some other way. And I think they really need some help, because it's such an important decision.

Story 2: As told to her next-door neighbour's 10-year-old son

When you finish school, you might want to carry on learning by going to college. It can be more fun than school if you choose the right course and the right place to go. One that suits you. And my job is going to be to help school leavers make the right choice. I am going to write a book to help them choose.

Story 3: As told to a school teacher

School leavers often want to apply for further education, but the wrong course at the wrong place can be disastrous – expensive and wasteful. Even if they know what they want, they don't know what FE colleges could offer them. I really want to work with students to get them to think clearly about what kind of next step will be best for them and whether that includes going to college. I understand what kind of options there are for them, what kind of courses and what kinds of colleges, and I've seen good and bad choices – I really want to encourage them to make a choice that will help them prosper in life.

Appealing words and ideas: whether to go to college, where to go, what it could it offer them, encourage, choices, understand, prosper.

Final draft purpose statement: *I serve the purpose of encouraging school students to understand what college could offer them and to make wise choices about whether and where to go to college, so that they can prosper in life.*

EXTENSION IDEAS

- This exercise works well if you do it as a group with some close friends and swap notes about what you have written. Actually telling each other the stories you have written – literally reading them out loud – allows others to help you get to the heart of what you are trying to say.

- The exercise also works if, instead of focusing on different kinds of listener, you deliberately choose a different kind of format to tell your story. For example, you could try writing a short piece of science fiction, or a fairy tale, or a piece of historical fiction about you as you might have been in the past. This may sound an absurd idea, but the only purpose of the exercise is to force yourself to generate different versions of your story without treating the exercise as a question in an examination.

FIGURE 5.1 Purpose worksheet

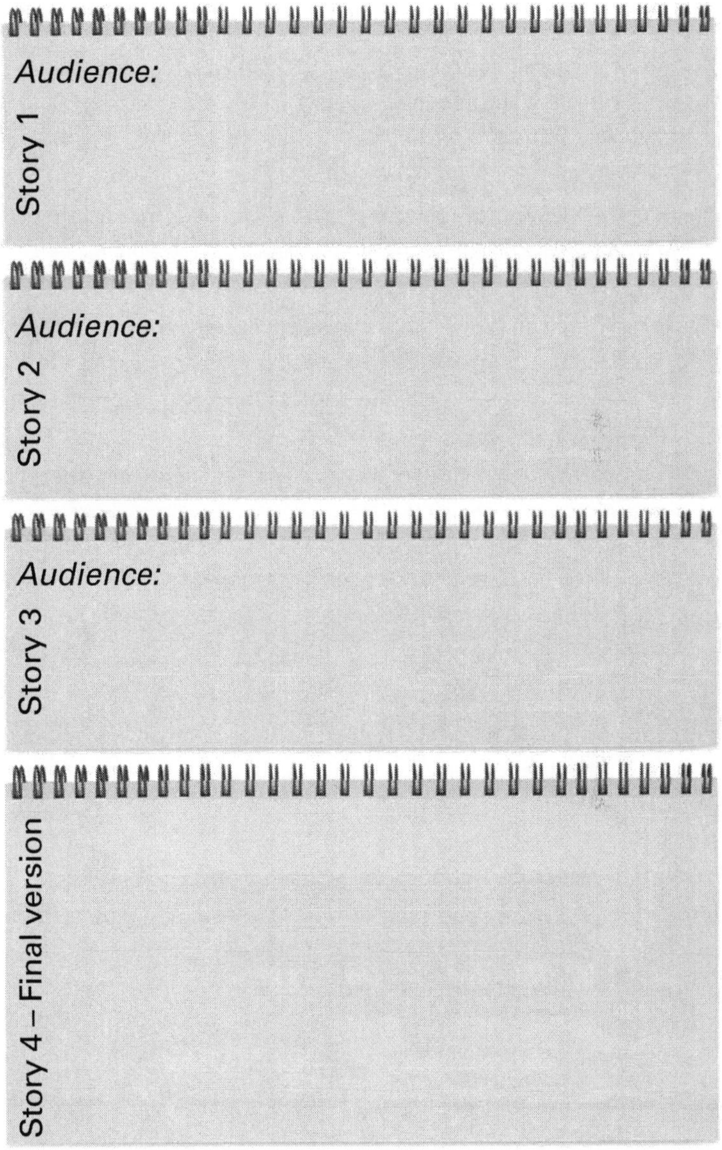

Story 1

Audience:

Story 2

Audience:

Story 3

Audience:

Story 4 – Final version

SUMMARY

- A statement of the purpose you serve will focus your strategy for your career, and will help you to shape your future direction. It will be as useful for you as it is for corporations: it will motivate you, help you to organize your life, and choose which opportunities to take or to turn down.

- Conversations about our purpose have long been part of individual coaching, and they are becoming more significant in corporate strategy, as regulators start to ask for statements of purpose which are coherent with what companies actually do.

- This history of organizations shows that purpose changes over time. The question for you is: what's your purpose in this phase of your working life?

- Because it's not an easy question to answer, the exercise gets you to create three different and very short stories about what you do and why. When you read them back to yourself, you will see some ideas and observations that resonate so strongly that you know you have articulated something that's part of your purpose statement.

What's next?

Now that you have a rough draft of your purpose statement, or some elements of it, the next step is to use it in your strategy work. Purpose statements are supposed to be organizing principles and that's what the next chapter is about.

CHAPTER SIX

Organizing your working life: your life architecture

This chapter is about deliberately organizing your life around your purpose. How can you make it as easy as possible to achieve your goals and get where you want to go?

Why this matters to you

Being clear about your purpose is useful, but organizing your life properly around it can be transformational. This isn't about devoting the whole of your life to your work, but rather a design challenge about the conscious choices you might make in setting yourself up for success. And there is more you can do on this than you might think, as the exercise will show you – women find that even small changes can make their working lives both easier and more successful, without compromising on their home life.

You usually know when your life *isn't* organized properly. Things feel out of kilter, and harder than they should be. Maybe you don't have the equipment that you need to work well with your remote team, or maybe it's about making more time to go on a really useful training course. Maybe the midweek conflict between a regular meeting and the need to get the children collected from school is wearing you out. You might be surprised that a book about career strategy covers such matters as the kind of IT equipment you use, or your weekly meeting schedule. But whether they are large or small choices, their effect can be significant, positively or negatively.

And there is a surprisingly long list of choices that you can make. The phrase 'life architecture' in the title of this chapter is a metaphor: a building is designed with supporting structures, energy, water and even a drainage system, as well as door handles and light switches. Now extend the metaphor to your life, and the point is obvious: there is a whole range of aspects of your life which you might alter, introduce or abandon. Building some new, small, daily habits or dropping some old ones might make a real difference in your working journey. So what might you change and how might you change it? That's what this chapter is about. Most women find that this is one of the most useful exercises in building their strategy, but it is also one of the hardest and it usually takes several attempts and multiple drafts. So don't worry if this seems too complicated at first – the effort will be worth it. This exercise will give you some clarity on how to get to where you want to go, and on the actions you'll need to take.

The idea

The idea of organizing your life around what you are trying to achieve – your purpose – seems, on the face of it, completely obvious. Why wouldn't you do that? Organizations try to do this, as we'll see later in this chapter. Business schools teach leaders how to design their organization architecture. But, for us, this is about *life* architecture. The exercise will invite you to explore the logical alignment between almost every aspect of your particular working life, even the tiny ones. That's what makes it both demanding and yet really useful.

The Purpose Alignment model does what it says in the title: it gets you to set out the direct and logical linkage between your purpose and your resources – between what you are trying to achieve and how you go about it. The model also reminds you to consider how your various stakeholders are involved in your life, who they are and what they want from you. Using this model will help you to take the statement of purpose that you developed in the previous chapter and play out its logical consequences for the way you set up your working life. You'll do this in a series of stages, since the model has a number of layers, with your purpose statement at the heart of it. To make this clearer, Figure 6.1 shows the idea in the form of a diagram.

You can see that the diagram illustrates the main point: for sustainable success, everything has to be logically aligned around your purpose. In some ways, the most important part of the diagram is the straight line which links each component. Following that logic, here's an outline of each layer of the model and what it comprises.

Layer 1: Your purpose in your context

First, the model helps you to test whether your purpose statement is realistic given your context. You can do that by looking at your various **stakeholders** both at work and outside. For most of us, they will usually be some combination of the following: colleagues, including: your boss; customers, including internal customers; your 'clan' – family and friends; and your community. Their needs and requirements are often very significant in women's lives, given the many roles we play and the range of responsibilities we have at work and outside. So it's worth being clear about what your stakeholders want from you,

FIGURE 6.1 The Purpose Alignment model

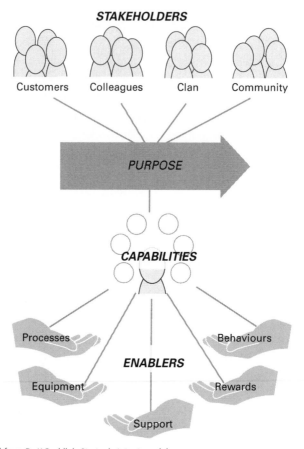

Adapted from Dr K Ruddle's Strategic Intent model.

and when. Does your purpose statement cover those requirements? It may need some adjustment if not. To be clear: it's not that the statement of purpose is entirely focused on what stakeholders want, but rather that their requirements are often a constraint within which we must work. Your rewriting shouldn't change your statement radically, but it might help you to make it more realizable. Here's an example of this point.

CASE STUDY   A small but significant change in Norah's statement
             of purpose

Norah ran the PR and communications function for a major utility based
in her home town, a job which she loved. She worked with the board
and senior management teams, dealing with a whole range of
marketing campaigns as well as responding to various issues which
arose locally and nationally. As a single mother, she also wanted to
support her son's school, and so, in her own time, she helped with
marketing and newsletters for the parent–teacher association.
Sometimes, the school's board of governors asked for her help, too, on
a voluntary basis. The first draft of her purpose statement was simple
and clear: '*I serve the purpose of providing strategic communications
advice*.' That certainly covered her professional work, both paid and
unpaid. But then she realized that this concise purpose statement didn't
quite cover all her stakeholders and their needs: her son needed her to
provide for them both financially. So she added one word to her
purpose statement to remind herself that, much as she loved using her
skills and experience wherever she could, her work – or some of it –
had to be *remunerated*. She had to balance the voluntary work she did
with her paid work, and that was a useful focus for her strategy.

Layer 2: Your purpose and you

The second layer of the model is about **capabilities**. What do you
have to be good at, in order to make your purpose real? What
skills or knowledge do you need to make the logic in the model
work? At this point, we are not asking whether or not you
currently have those capabilities right now, since we'll come to
that in Chapter 7.

Layer 3: Your purpose and the logistics of your life

Third, you'll look at how you could organize your life to make
sure that you can sustain these necessary capabilities. This will
take you down into the **enablers**, the logistics of your working
life and what supporting arrangements you have outside work

for your other commitments. For example, how far you have to commute, who organizes your diary, how much holiday you take, how you reward yourself, or how much extra help you might need at home.

Logical alignment

As we've said, these layers are linked together by the line of logic between what you want to achieve (your purpose) and what you need to put in place to allow that to happen. You can get at this logic through a series of questions, with an 'if... then...' construction:

- **First layer:** What do your stakeholders want from you? *If* this is what they want from you, *then* does your statement of purpose cover this?
- **Second layer:** *If* this is the purpose you serve, *then* what capabilities, skills and knowledge do you need? What do you need to be good at?
- **Third layer:** *If* you want to build and sustain those skills and capabilities, *then* what other enablers or support structures do you need to make this life architecture work?

Here's an example of how this exercise can help you to see the logical implications of your purpose statement. When Maddy did this exercise, her analysis gave her a useful insight about the capabilities she would need if she wanted to continue to do the kind of work she specialized in.

CASE STUDY   What Maddy needs to be good at

Maddy talked about her job with a mixture of enthusiasm and frustration. She specialized in working on innovative IT projects, using the very latest technology. One of the reasons she loved the work was that she could shape her job the way she wanted, deciding for herself what to focus on. The technology was so new that there were very few patterns to follow. But her frustrations were evident, too. The university where she worked was often unwilling to give her team enough budget to make the most of the new approaches. The constant need to try to persuade and influence the organization to invest had begun to affect her confidence. And she had a nagging sense that she wasn't really valued by her employers, even though she worked hard on areas that were actually vital to the university's future. When she drew her Journey Map, she'd seen the same problem occurring repeatedly: involvement in something new and leading edge, with increasingly useful applications, and then the stress of having to argue for the right resources or even for a salary increase.

Working through the Purpose Alignment exercise gave her a light-bulb moment: because the work she loved to do was always at the leading edge of technology, her employers rarely understood what she did. They were often slow to see its significance and therefore couldn't see the need for more resource in this area – and, on a personal level, to reward and promote her. In other words, the frustration she felt at constantly having to persuade her boss to fund the work and to pay her team properly for their skills was part and parcel of the kind of new and innovative work she loved to do. To put it in terms of the exercise: *if* she wanted to continue working in leading-edge technology, *then* she would have to continue to argue for resources to invest in technology which she understood well, but her employers did not. With this insight, she realized that, for her, a key capability would always be her influencing skills. This in turn gave her a clue to some immediate actions: strengthening her influence within the university by getting more involved in faculty initiatives, demonstrating her understanding of teaching and learning needs, and taking every opportunity to explain how the new technology could help.

Maddy's first-draft Purpose Alignment model looked like this:

FIGURE 6.2 Maddy's worksheet

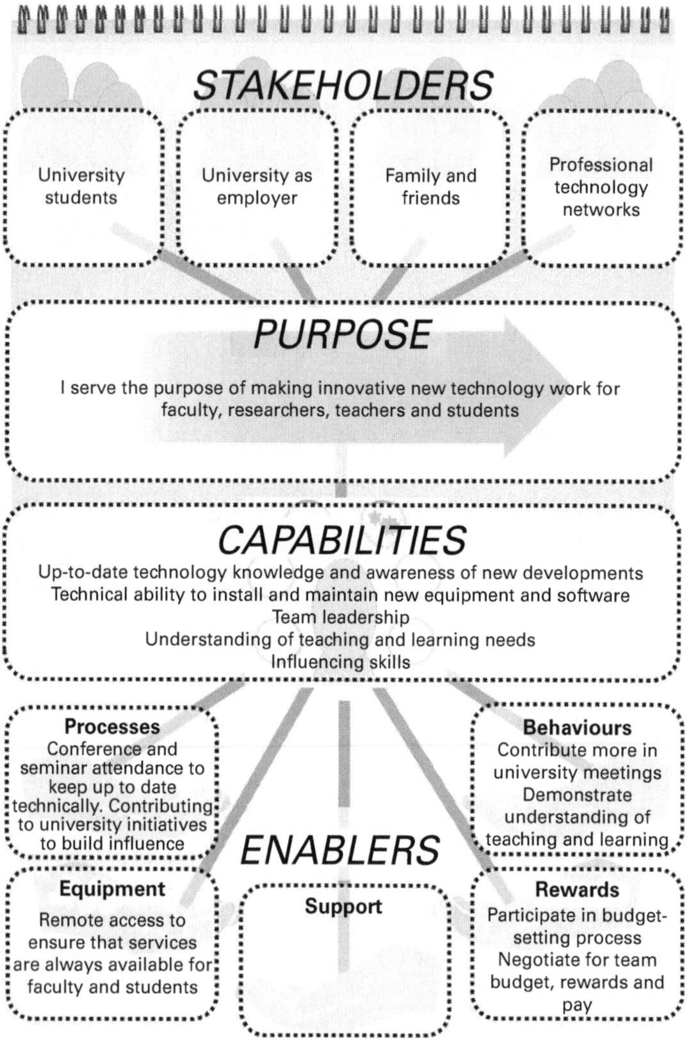

STAKEHOLDERS

| University students | University as employer | Family and friends | Professional technology networks |

PURPOSE

I serve the purpose of making innovative new technology work for faculty, researchers, teachers and students

CAPABILITIES

Up-to-date technology knowledge and awareness of new developments
Technical ability to install and maintain new equipment and software
Team leadership
Understanding of teaching and learning needs
Influencing skills

Processes
Conference and seminar attendance to keep up to date technically. Contributing to university initiatives to build influence

Behaviours
Contribute more in university meetings
Demonstrate understanding of teaching and learning

ENABLERS

Equipment
Remote access to ensure that services are always available for faculty and students

Support

Rewards
Participate in budget-setting process
Negotiate for team budget, rewards and pay

Parallels with corporate strategy

For many years, I've worked with organizations on the idea of strategic alignment, using some concepts developed from research by a colleague of mine, Dr Keith Ruddle. His work illustrates the logical and necessary connection between an organization's strategic intent and all the other aspects: capabilities and skills, processes, physical infrastructure, information assets, management styles, the way people are hired, paid and fired, and the kind of culture that operates. He summarizes his work in this model, similar to the one we use here, but for an organizational context:

FIGURE 6.3   The Purpose Alignment model for organizations

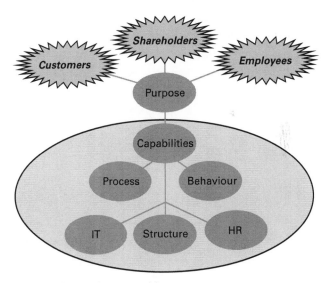

Source: Dr K Ruddle's Strategic Intent model.

Two examples: organizations that sell food

In teaching this model, we often use two examples of organizations which both sell food. The first case example is McDonald's. You may not choose to eat there every day, but it provides consistent, affordable food with a guaranteed level of quality in a convenient location. McDonald's is successful because it can replicate its systems and processes to deliver a standardized range of products at the right price in many different locations throughout the world. Approximately 69 million people eat at McDonald's each day, around 1 per cent of the world's population. In order to do this so successfully and at such scale, the organization has several really distinctive capabilities. They know how to design and implement standardized, scalable processes to maximize the efficiency of what they do. They are able to implement these processes through a franchise operation, given that more than 90 per cent of their restaurants are owner-managed. Their logistics and procurement processes are tightly controlled to help them to operate at scale across multiple locations. Staff recruitment is efficient and quick: you have to apply online and could be in post within two weeks. Once employed, the organization is very good at training all sorts of people – for example, students, apprentices, retirees – to perform routine tasks expertly. It is said that within an hour of starting work, a new employee at a McDonald's operation can be doing something useful. Do they offer world-class, individualized service? No, although the service is perfectly acceptable, because that is not what they are trying to offer and that is not what they are organized to do. McDonald's has chosen a purpose which is about efficient delivery of a product at a quality, price and location which families, people on the move or anyone who is hungry will want. And they've designed every single aspect of their organization accordingly.

Take a different kind of food experience: Belmond Le Manoir aux Quat'Saisons in Oxfordshire provides food too, but its purpose is quite different. It's based in a beautiful country house, with glorious grounds. You might go there for a special celebration, hoping for a very luxurious experience along with delicious food. And that is what you get, because the organization has been carefully designed around the delivery of that purpose.

In order to provide a level of service that is way beyond what you would normally expect in a restaurant or hotel, staff are chosen for their service orientation. The organization embodies this even in the way they recruit, holding open days at the hotel for prospective employees, so that potential staff see from the start that 'the good does not interest us, the sublime does', as it says on the website. The hotel has won numerous awards for recruitment and student placement initiatives and has a Twitter account specifically for recruitment. Once appointed, staff are given the discretion to provide a service tailored to each customer. If you go there for lunch with a set of allergies, you will be given your own printed menu, specifically designed with a selection of dishes chosen for you. If you don't like where you are sitting in the restaurant, the first member of staff you encounter will help you to move, without asking any further questions or seeking higher authority from a manager. The culture of the organization encourages staff to respond to customer needs almost whatever they may be. And their reward systems have been designed to foster that focus on service: after a year's employment and every year thereafter, members of staff are rewarded with a guest experience themselves. This luxurious perk has the benefit of allowing them to see what it is like to be a guest at Le Manoir themselves – to experience the service as their customers do. It's not just a valuable reward, but a training and development opportunity too.

These two different organizations have chosen very different purposes and set themselves up accordingly. They've paid attention to every aspect of how they work – whether that's recruitment, training, staff incentives or procurement processes. That's why they are successful. But if they changed their purpose, they'd have to redesign much of what they do, because their current ways of working serve their current purpose.

The underlying research

When an organization develops a new strategy, there is a considerable amount of work done on related plans for other parts of the business, because strategy reviews often precipitate a whole raft of internal changes. The Purpose Alignment model sets the agenda for change: to sort out exactly what will need to be altered if the organization wants to do something new or to move into a different market. This might include office moves or investment in new digital support systems; perhaps the staff benefits scheme is to be restructured, or a new executive development programme commissioned to support the delivery of the new strategy. This set of processes is about the organization architecture: getting the various aspects and elements organized logically to support the realization of the long-term purpose, as set out in the strategic plan.

In his book *Align: A leadership blueprint for aligning enterprise purpose, strategy and organisation*, Professor Jonathan Trevor underlines the importance of this in corporate contexts: 'the best-aligned enterprises are the best performing because their leaders approach alignment as a strategic concern'. Organizational leaders often fail to make the right choices about exactly how their organization works because they haven't seen the significance of some of those smaller local decisions and processes. Employees, by contrast, often notice the illogical and inconsistent ways the organization works given the statement of purpose that is in the annual report. You may have seen this yourself: the business that says it values training and development for staff very highly but will cancel your attendance on a programme at the drop of a hat; or the company that prides itself on trusting its staff but won't implement flexible working arrangements because people might take advantage of them.

Recognizing the significance of these smaller choices and decisions is half the battle; as we saw in the Strategy Triangle model, the connection between purpose and resources is vital in a balanced, workable strategy.

As you start to think about applying this to your own working life, here's an example of how the model helped Rhiannon – who you'll remember from the previous chapter was working in a college of further education – as she made a major change in her own strategy.

CASE STUDY   Getting organized around a new purpose

Once she had drafted her new purpose statement, Rhiannon was relieved to see that the Purpose Alignment exercise could help her to see how to make it real. Her plans to make some quite significant changes in her working life – such as moving from working in one college to writing a book about opportunities in all colleges – seemed exciting but also made her nervous. She admitted to herself that she had some of the capabilities she needed, but not all of them. And there were some gaps in her knowledge, too. That's why she started volunteering in schools, helping students going through the college application process. Building the right capabilities was a good place to start in implementing her new strategy.

As she worked through the exercise, she could see that this big change of direction would require a whole raft of other smaller changes in her 'life architecture'. First, managing her time: she didn't think she could write the book while working full-time, so she started negotiations with her current employers to agree some part-time duties just for one academic year. She'd probably work from home to write the book, but she had none of the facilities she needed to do this – particularly a reliable computer and printer in a dedicated office space. Since her IT skills were basic, she decided to outsource this and found a small local firm to help her.

The exercise helped her to imagine what it would be like to work from home, and she began to be concerned that she might feel rather isolated. So finding a network of other writers to talk to and get advice from would be useful. And finally, since money would be tight for the next year, she could see that she had to give more thought to the idea of some small, low-cost rewards to keep her motivated in implementing her new strategy.

Here's what her Purpose Alignment diagram looked like:

FIGURE 6.4 Rhiannon's worksheet

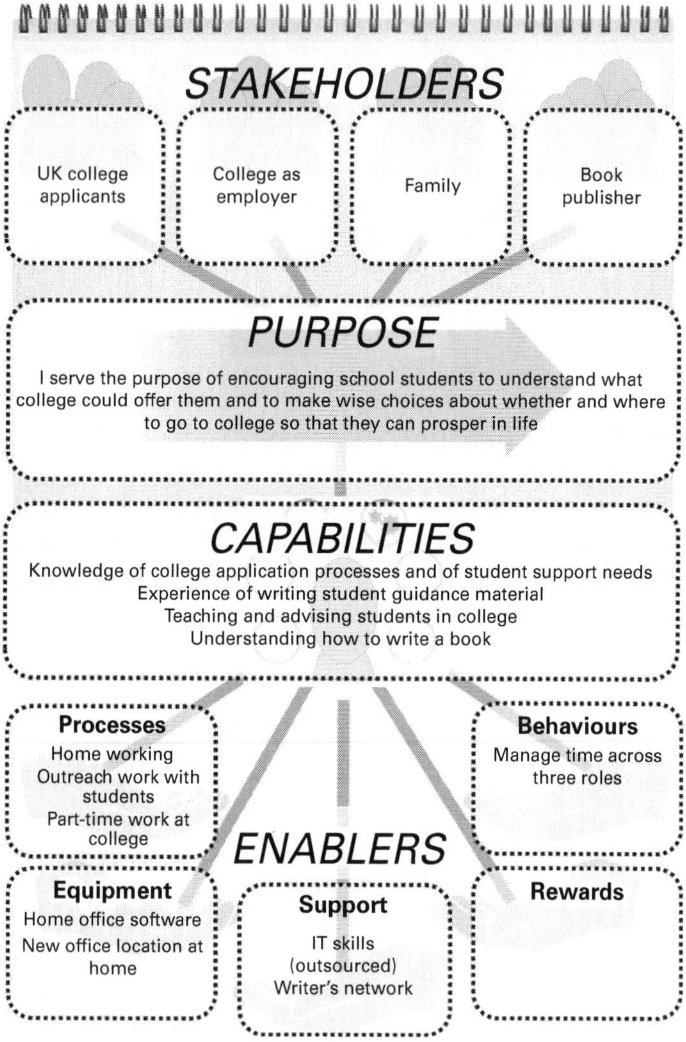

STAKEHOLDERS

UK college applicants

College as employer

Family

Book publisher

PURPOSE

I serve the purpose of encouraging school students to understand what college could offer them and to make wise choices about whether and where to go to college so that they can prosper in life

CAPABILITIES

Knowledge of college application processes and of student support needs
Experience of writing student guidance material
Teaching and advising students in college
Understanding how to write a book

Processes
Home working
Outreach work with students
Part-time work at college

Behaviours
Manage time across three roles

ENABLERS

Equipment
Home office software
New office location at home

Support
IT skills (outsourced)
Writer's network

Rewards

The exercise: guidance

Use the worksheet at the end of this chapter to help structure your thinking as you go through each step.

Step 1

Take the purpose statement which you drafted in the previous chapter and write that in the central box labelled 'Purpose' on the worksheet. This will be the keystone for your analysis of the way you want to organize your working life.

Step 2

At the top of the worksheet, list all the stakeholders in your world who need something from you. This will include your boss and colleagues at work, but should also include people outside work – your family, or the community groups you volunteer with, or other people you care for. Although this book is about your working life, it has to fit into the context of the whole of your life, and that includes responsibilities you have and roles you play outside work. The list might also include your customers, particularly if you work for yourself. You might also want to write down what it is that each stakeholder needs from you: maybe your expertise, your time, your support or the money you earn to keep them fed and clothed.

Step 3

Now take a look at the logical alignment so far: does your purpose statement accommodate what your various stakeholders need from you? Ask yourself: if they need this, then does your purpose statement meet those needs? If not, could you tweak your purpose statement a little to solve that mismatch? Or is it so different that you need to rethink things? (In which case, go back to the exercise in Chapter 5 and have another go at writing a story which is about both what you *want* to do and what you *have* to do to meet the needs of those who rely on you.)

Step 4

Once you are satisfied that the purpose statement is logical given your context, ask yourself: if I want to achieve this purpose, then what do I have to be good at? That's what the 'Capabilities' box is for: listing those capabilities, skills and knowledge which you must have to achieve your purpose. This is not just about the capabilities you already have; it might be about some that you are missing or need to develop.

Step 5

Now you have a list of the capabilities you need to make this purpose a reality, what else do you need in your life to keep those skills up to date or to acquire or develop the new ones that you need? If you were doing this analysis in an organizational context, you would consider the following aspects: processes, behaviours, organizational structures, IT and enabling equipment, and pay and reward systems. When we think about our life architecture, we can use broadly the same categories:

- **Processes:** What regular processes do you need personally to make sure that this works? (For example, managing your own diary instead of allowing someone else to do it for you? Or maybe the other way round?)

- **Behaviours:** Do you need to change what you do? (For example, cutting down on an external activity like your membership of a singing group for the rest of the year?)

- **Equipment:** What would make your working life easier? (For example, creating space at home so that you can work efficiently there if you need to? A better scanner to digitize material quickly?)

- **Support outside work:** What could you put in place to help you? (For example, an agreement with a neighbour that your children might go to her house to play one afternoon a week?)
- **Rewards:** This is about both your financial situation and the other rewards that you could give yourself to maintain your motivation. (For example, an afternoon off once a month, just for you.)

This part of the exercise is about literally anything that you feel you need to build into your life to make your purpose real. In the figure below, there are some examples of other enablers that you might want to consider, just as suggestions.

FIGURE 6.5 Example enablers

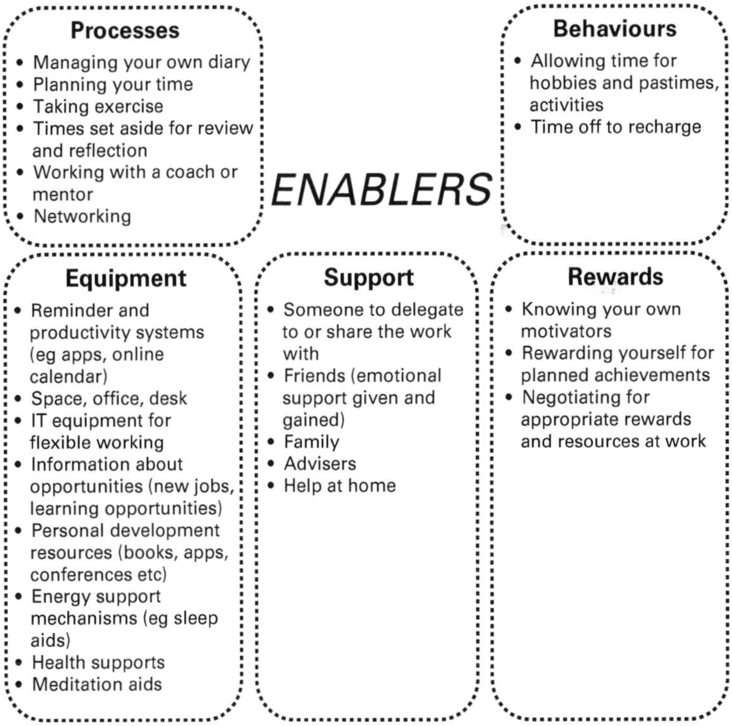

Processes
- Managing your own diary
- Planning your time
- Taking exercise
- Times set aside for review and reflection
- Working with a coach or mentor
- Networking

Behaviours
- Allowing time for hobbies and pastimes, activities
- Time off to recharge

ENABLERS

Equipment
- Reminder and productivity systems (eg apps, online calendar)
- Space, office, desk
- IT equipment for flexible working
- Information about opportunities (new jobs, learning opportunities)
- Personal development resources (books, apps, conferences etc)
- Energy support mechanisms (eg sleep aids)
- Health supports
- Meditation aids

Support
- Someone to delegate to or share the work with
- Friends (emotional support given and gained)
- Family
- Advisers
- Help at home

Rewards
- Knowing your own motivators
- Rewarding yourself for planned achievements
- Negotiating for appropriate rewards and resources at work

As you start work on your own analysis using the worksheet, here is an example of the analysis that Norah did, once she had made a slight alteration in her purpose statement.

CASE STUDY   Norah's Purpose Alignment exercise

Norah had already recognized that her purpose statement had to address the need to support her family. But when she completed the exercise, she could see more clearly what wasn't working, what was out of alignment. First, money: although she worked full-time, the cost of childcare for her son in the school holidays ate up much of her income. Second, she felt she had to keep her skills up to date and her professional networks alive, as an insurance policy for future employment. And she had to do this while still delivering good results at work. The problem seemed to come down to time and how she used it, at work and outside.

She decided that one option would be to negotiate a new annualized hours work contract, just for the next two years, until her son went to secondary school. If she could work reduced hours during the school holidays in exchange for increased hours during the school terms, she could spend less on school holiday childcare. She might even find time for her own professional development. It sounded like a good plan in theory, but she knew she would need some good negotiation skills to make it work. Obviously, she'd need to negotiate with her boss, but she'd also need to get better at making arrangements with colleagues about deadlines and work allocation given her new schedule. None of this looked easy. But she could at least get started, by agreeing with another parent that they would share the school drop-off in the mornings so that, on some days, she could make an early start. She also began to look for an online negotiation programme, to help her to agree a new contract with her boss.

Here's what her Purpose Alignment worksheet looked like at this point in her thinking. It wasn't complete, but she could already see what she might do next.

FIGURE 6.6 Norah's worksheet

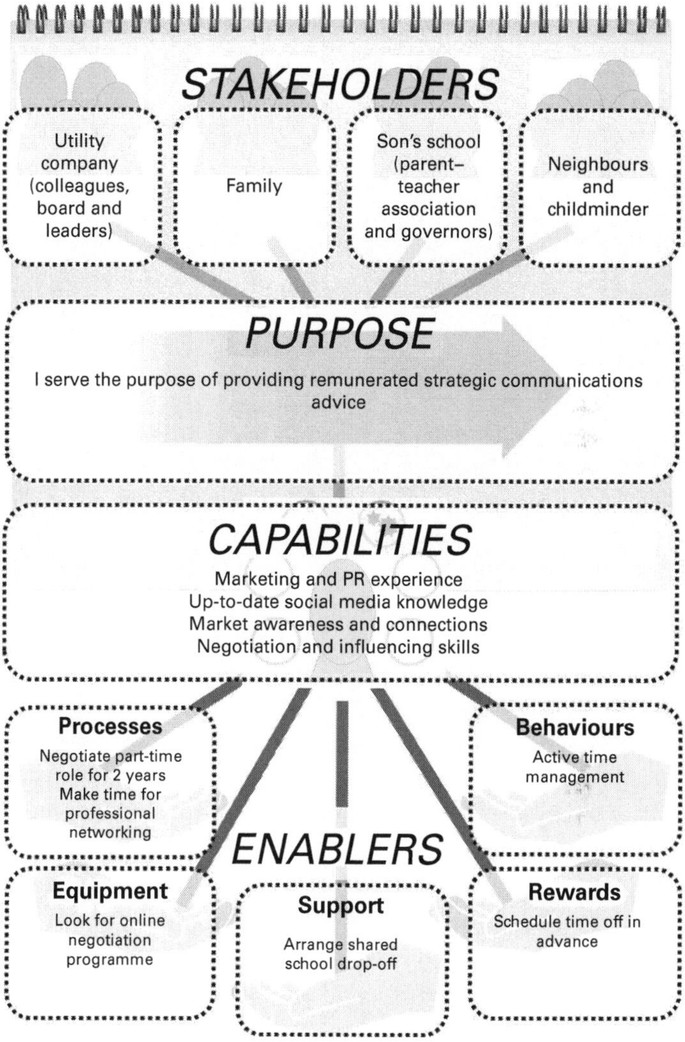

STAKEHOLDERS

Utility company (colleagues, board and leaders)

Family

Son's school (parent–teacher association and governors)

Neighbours and childminder

PURPOSE

I serve the purpose of providing remunerated strategic communications advice

CAPABILITIES

Marketing and PR experience
Up-to-date social media knowledge
Market awareness and connections
Negotiation and influencing skills

Processes

Negotiate part-time role for 2 years
Make time for professional networking

Behaviours

Active time management

ENABLERS

Equipment

Look for online negotiation programme

Support

Arrange shared school drop-off

Rewards

Schedule time off in advance

EXTENSION IDEAS

- Try redoing this exercise with a slightly different version of your purpose statement from Chapter 5. This is particularly useful if you are not certain that you have your purpose statement quite right yet, since it still allows you to make some progress. See what, if any, difference it makes to the way in which you might structure the rest of your life.

- If you found in Step 3 that your stakeholders really do want more and different things from you than any one human can provide, you might need to plan for some negotiation with them, or find some different ways of meeting those requirements.

- Since this model works in layers, you can develop it either from the top down, thinking about stakeholders first – as in the guidance – or by starting with your capabilities. There is an 'explore' aspect to strategy – looking outside to your stakeholders and their requirements and thinking from the outside in – as well as an 'exploit' dimension which focuses on the resources you already have and how you might use them more effectively. If you find that you are not quite satisfied with your purpose statement as the foundation stone for this analysis, try starting with the capabilities and skills you already have and work up through the model to think about how you might use them, and down to consider how you might sustain them.

- Don't forget to consider how you will reward yourself as you implement your strategy. That might be the small rewards which energize and motivate you or a reminder to prepare properly for formal salary review or bonus discussions at work. Or both.

SUMMARY

- Organizing your life around your purpose will help you to achieve it. In the corporate world, a new strategy usually requires the organization architecture to be redesigned accordingly, and that's true for us as individuals, too.
- The Purpose Alignment model takes your statement of purpose and asks you to draw out the logical consequences for your life, using a series of 'if... then...' questions.
- First, look at what your various stakeholders at work and outside need from you and compare this with your purpose statement. *If* this is what your stakeholders want and need, *then* does your purpose statement accommodate this? If not, you will either need to tweak your purpose statement or negotiate with some stakeholders to find another way of meeting their needs.
- The second step is to be clear about the capabilities you need. *If* you want to achieve your purpose, *then* what do you have to be good at? What skills and knowledge do you need?
- Next, look at your life architecture: *if* you want to sustain these capabilities and make it as easy as possible for you to achieve your purpose, *then* what else do you need? This might involve changing processes, behaviours and habits, acquiring better equipment or even reviewing your finances.

What's next?

If you've done the exercise in this chapter, one of your conclusions will be about the list of key capabilities you feel you need to make your purpose real. So now the question is whether or not you already have those capabilities. And, if not, what then? That's what Chapter 7 is about.

FIGURE 6.7 Purpose Alignment worksheet

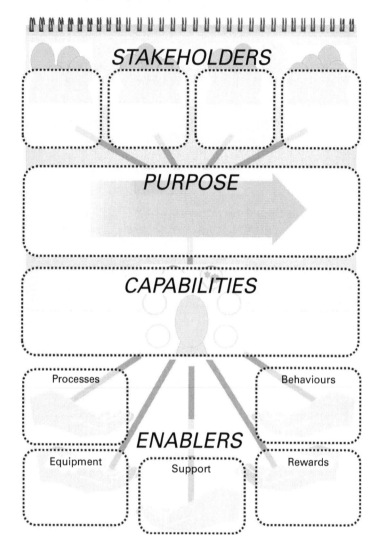

CHAPTER SEVEN

What's worth developing

The Strengths model

Do you have the capabilities you need to realize your purpose?
Are they sufficiently strong? If not, what's the best way to
develop them?

Why this matters to you

In a book about developing your career, you would expect there
to be a chapter about self-development. We all have some of the
skills we need and some that are perhaps not as strong as we
would like. The ability to learn and develop is vital for a successful working life in a world which changes all the time. And, as
we know, learning is good for the brain and our mental health as
we grow older.

At school and at work, the prevailing idea about our performance is that we have some strengths – things we do well – and some weaknesses – things which we are told we need to improve. This simple bifurcation between what we are 'good at' and what we are, apparently, 'not good at' prevents us from seeing some more useful approaches to self-development. The trouble is that going on a training course to overcome a weakness isn't much fun – and it doesn't really work either. And we are almost never sent on a training course to make an existing strength even stronger. So the ideas in this chapter offer some new options. Many people find these new approaches both liberating and energizing, and women seem to find them particularly useful. This might be because we find we have time constraints and this approach can give some real focus to what we decide to do. It might also be because it reminds us that we have a whole range of strengths which are worth investing in and using to the full at work.

The idea

The idea in this chapter moves beyond the simple categorization of capabilities as either strong or weak. Instead of merely assessing capability against a single competence scale – 'How good am I at this?' – this model suggests that you should also look at a second scale: does this capability fit with your psychometric preferences or not? Are there aspects of your personality which help you to develop this capability? If not, this might explain why it is harder for you to strengthen a particular capability and become really good at it. Harder, but not always impossible. Thinking about the capabilities you use on *both* scales, not just assessing current levels of skill, will give you a wider set of strategies to develop them.

The best way to visualize this is with a diagram (see Figure 7.1).

FIGURE 7.1   The Strengths model

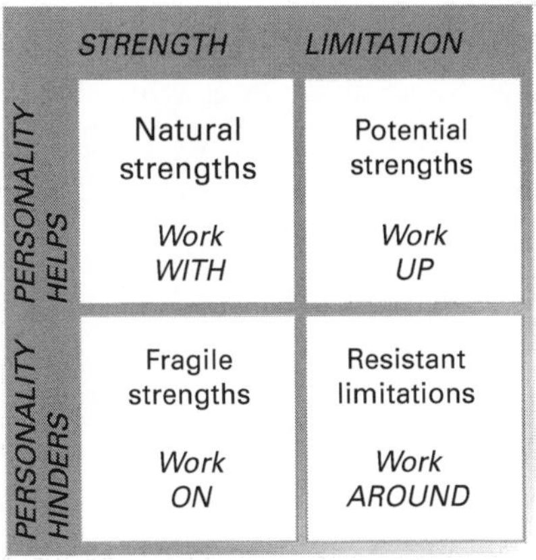

	STRENGTH	LIMITATION
PERSONALITY HELPS	Natural strengths *Work* *WITH*	Potential strengths *Work* *UP*
PERSONALITY HINDERS	Fragile strengths *Work* *ON*	Resistant limitations *Work* *AROUND*

Source: Dr David Pendleton

This model has two axes: the horizontal axis along the top shows how strong your capabilities are, from strong on the left to less strong at the right-hand end. The second dimension, the vertical axis, is about personality: whether those psychometric preferences that are part of who we are will help you or hinder you in being good at a particular task. The idea is that we are likely to be good at some things and to find some others more difficult, not because we haven't been trained or are not trying, but just because our psychometric preferences make it hard to excel at some tasks. For example, many extroverts find it hard to think and work in silence for long, because they like to do their thinking while moving their lips, talking out loud. They have a preference for working with other people. It doesn't mean they are incapable of working in silence on their own, but it doesn't come naturally to them.

In other words, our capabilities are a blend of ability and psychological preference. They are not simply a strength or a weakness, but a much more nuanced set of strengths and limitations. The model's two dimensions help us to see our capabilities more clearly and to decide, therefore, what's the best development route in each case.

Capabilities and strategies for development

The first and most obvious category in the model is the idea of **natural strengths**: those capabilities which score highly on both dimensions. You'll know that you are good at these things from feedback which you have had over the years. You'll also feel that they are congruent with your personality simply because you like using these skills. It's quite likely that these natural strengths have always been obvious to you and others since they fit with your preferences. The idea is that we should work *with* our natural strengths, exploit them, and find opportunities to use them at work, because we are good at them. Those are the capabilities which might make you famous, at least in your team. If you have work which allows you to use those natural strengths every day, the chances are that you will enjoy your job.

The second category, though, is those capabilities we have which are not that strong but which in theory we should be good at, because they fit with our personality preferences. The model calls these **potential strengths** and suggests that we should *work these up*. They are worth investing development energy in because, in theory, given our personality preferences, we could become much better in these areas. For example, if you are very sociable and enjoy talking to people but your presentation skills are not that strong, you might benefit greatly from some training in this area, to turn your potential strength into a natural strength.

The third category covers the capabilities you have developed over the years because your roles demand them, but which you continue to find difficult. Often, this is because they don't really fit with your personality preferences. The model refers to these as **fragile strengths**: because they don't really fit with the kind of person you are, you have to keep putting in lots of effort and energy to sustain your performance. In other words, you have to *work on* these areas in order to sustain them. You can often get an easy clue to which are your fragile strengths when you consider those things that you do regularly at work and are quite good at but don't really enjoy.

The final category refers to those capabilities which are not strong at all, and which are not congruent with the personality preferences you have. You'll probably know exactly which these are since they will have been appearing on your school reports and performance appraisals for years. This model doesn't refer to these as weaknesses, but as **resistant limitations**. Our capabilities are weak in these areas precisely because we are temperamentally unsuited to tasks which require them. No matter how hard we try, we never really improve. So the strategy for your development in these areas is very different: *work around* them.

By 'work around', we mean a strategy of collaboration with someone else. This is a truly liberating idea which will change the way you think about your self-development as well as the kind of job you do. It frees you from the feeling that you have to be good at everything; you don't have to be the perfectly well-rounded leader who can do everything in her job description brilliantly. Actually, that's a psychologically impossible idea. But it is possible to build a well-rounded team of people who can collaborate with each other constructively to make the best use of everybody's natural strengths. There comes a stage in your life when you don't need to go on yet another course, investing time, energy and money in trying once again to overcome a 'weakness' which is part of who you are. Instead, focus on working with someone who has a great talent in this area. They will enjoy using their natural strength and you will benefit from working with them.

Figure 7.2 shows an illustration of this 'work around' strategy.

FIGURE 7.2 Work-around strategy: collaboration

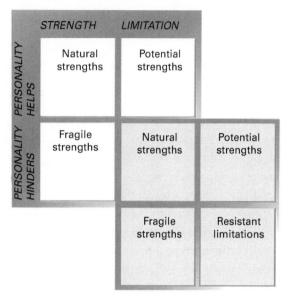

Source Dr David Pendleton

To show how this works in practice, here's Emma's story.

CASE STUDY Emma's work-around

Emma was the project director for a large transformation project designed to save £10 million of annual operating costs for a financial services business. The work was going well, and Emma had begun to feel that they were really on track, when it was suddenly announced that their business would be merging with another large organization. Despite that, Emma and her team were told that the project objective still had to be achieved. She saw a number of people roll their eyes when they were instructed to continue the work as planned, because they all knew that this was unrealistic. From then on, every day, she and the team had to make changes to the project design to be sure that the transformation would work for the new merged business. Sometimes they had to add to the scope of the work, while at other times they had to cut out whole areas of work. This was challenging but interesting, and Emma enjoyed the work since she had a psychometric preference for new ideas and large-scale issues – this was a natural strength for her. However, every design change had to be analysed to ensure that it didn't *add* cost when the objective was to *reduce* cost. This level of detailed financial scrutiny was definitely not one of Emma's strengths; the very characteristics that made her good at large design changes made her less able to do the detailed follow-through work. For a few weeks, she persevered in addressing her resistant limitation with little success and much frustration. Then she decided on a new approach: she negotiated with the finance team to assign an analyst from the department to work part-time on the project with the specific brief of keeping track of all the changes in scope and their financial implications. The analyst was glad to have the chance to work in a different area of the business and could see that this was important work. Emma commented about this arrangement: 'I agreed a kind of contract with her – that she would keep alerting me to financial implications even if sometimes it appeared that I wasn't listening. It worked: her financial scrutiny was better than mine but I knew enough to take her advice.'

As you can see from Emma's story, the model might get you to think differently about how you do your existing job and to explore ways of making better use of your strengths while working around your limitations. Take another example: one very able, introverted senior leader greatly disliked giving large presentations in the City but realized that this was an important part of her job. She decided that rather than doing all the talking herself, she would orchestrate a team presentation with board colleagues, allowing them to use their natural strengths. She was clearly the anchor and leader but didn't have to do much of the presenting.

This kind of work-around is not always possible, though. Another senior manager sighed heavily when she had explored her version of the Strengths model and said ruefully: 'Now I know why I have an ulcer – most of my job requires me to use my fragile strengths every single day.' The solution for her was to look for a different kind of role, one which allowed her to use her natural strengths.

So this model offers a wider range of choices for development, for job crafting and for your strategy. It opens up a range of choices about what you do now and what you might do in the future. Seeing clearly what kind of capabilities you have will help you to choose a realistic and comprehensive development approach. For example, you could choose to practise doing some new tasks in those areas of *potential* strength to see if you really can develop them into natural strengths. And if your job calls on your fragile strengths regularly, which require effort to sustain, you'll also need to find ways of sustaining your energy. In Stage 3, we will look at how you might turn these strategic insights into an implementable plan.

You can see why this analysis feels liberating: it's a gear change in your approach to self-development because it's based on your understanding of *why* you are good in some areas and less so in others – and what you might do about it. To put this in the context of the Strategy Triangle: the Strengths model helps to formulate your resource strategy and offers you a genuinely different set of choices about how to develop your capabilities to achieve a new purpose, or to seize a new opportunity, or both.

Parallels with corporate strategy

One of the traditional perspectives on strategy formulation uses the competence model to define precisely what the organization is good at and what critical areas of skill are lacking. That's not just an internal perspective, though, as the Strategy Triangle reminds us. The organization must have the right set of competences to achieve its purpose and it also has to find a market opportunity to make use of those competences. If the assessment of what's needed reveals some gaps, the organization has various options. The most obvious is to invest in development programmes for teams and leaders. This works well depending on what kind of capability is to be developed and whether the cultural context will actually allow those newly developed competences to be used in reality. A classic example is where a company seeks to be more innovative; development programmes to foster this can help, but if the organization doesn't tolerate errors or mistakes well, any attempts to do something innovative but risky will be squashed, and eventually people give up.

There are other options: for example, a company might choose to acquire or partner with another organization full of people who already have those skills, in an organizational version of the collaboration idea. Alternatively, organizations sometimes hire an individual or a team to inject their natural strengths into the business, as a teacher or catalyst. This might work in theory but it tends to be less successful in practice. Too often, the organization hasn't grasped what these new skills really mean for the way things are done or for the organization's culture. That's exactly the point made in the previous chapter: things can get out of alignment when you are trying to inject something new, unless you make some adjustments. It's true for individuals, too: every time there is a change in your purpose, or context, or when you move into a different phase of life, there will probably be a need to develop your skills in some areas.

The underlying research

The two-dimensional Strengths model explored in this chapter was developed by a colleague, Dr David Pendleton, a psychologist who has spent many years working with leaders all over the world. He specializes in psychometric research and much of his work is done using personality-profiling tools to help people develop their self-awareness, their sense of themselves. The point is that the very characteristics which make us excellent in some areas are also the characteristics that hinder us from being capable in other areas (Pendleton and Furnham, 2012). An ability to see new and innovative ideas, for example, is not often accompanied by strong abilities to oversee the details of an existing operational process – the wiring we have that makes us good at one thing will by definition prevent us from being good at the other. That's why a degree of self-awareness is the vital starting point for any self-development. This clear-eyed understanding of your own strengths and limitations, as well as your preferences, is the foundation for growth.

But self-acceptance is also key. Understanding and accepting who you are allows you to work with the grain of your personality rather than against it. And recognizing your strengths, without undue arrogance, allows you to focus on using and developing them to best effect in your working life, because they are the capabilities that will fuel your success.

So our job is to develop both self-awareness and self-acceptance. And we are responsible for our own development, nobody else – not our employers or our boss. When interviewed during the research work, successful women talked about making their own development plans, rather than waiting for a performance appraisal to point out that there was a skill gap. They prioritized development as a strategic choice, as part of owning their own career.

The exercise: guidance

There are several ways in which you can use this model to generate a map of your own strengths. The first and most obvious way is to use the insights from any psychometric profiling which you may have done in the past to help you with the personality preference dimension. The difficulty is, though, that this profile data does not necessarily correlate clearly with the capabilities you use at work.

So here is an easier way: use 'liking' as a proxy for psychometric preference. It's much easier to look at a list of the capabilities we have or are required to use at work and decide which ones we like doing and which we don't. It's not such a bad proxy either: most of us like doing things that feel interesting or come naturally to us, which may indicate that we are working with the grain of our personality rather than against it.

Step 1

The place to start is with a list of capabilities. You could take this from your performance appraisal system or you can use the questions on your last 360-degree feedback. Or you could simply look at your diary and list the capabilities you've used at work over the last month. I suggest that you start with a short list – around nine capabilities. Don't just list the things you like doing or are good at: list the things which you actually have to do in your job. Be sure to pick at least one capability which gets mentioned in your performance review meetings as an area to work on, so that you can use the model to see what kind of capability it is for you and what might be the best strategy to develop it.

Figure 7.3 shows a sample list of some of the capabilities that women have used over the past decade when experimenting with this exercise, just to help you to be clear about what we mean when we say 'capability'. And if all else fails, you could simply pick nine from this list, as long as they really are part of what you do at work.

Step 2

Now that you have chosen a list of nine capabilities which you actually use in your job, re-sequence that list, starting at the top

FIGURE 7.3 Sample capabilities

Sample capabilities

- Planning
- Delivering
- Communicating
- Leading your team
- Innovating
- Researching ideas, investigating
- Developing strategies
- Solving crises
- Managing people
- Reviewing quality
- Presenting
- Training, teaching
- Coaching
- Managing detail
- Numerical analysis
- Making decisions
- Setting standards

- Collaborating with others
- Brainstorming
- Selling
- Defining goals
- Managing processes
- Setting targets
- Measuring output
- Implementing changes
- Managing risk
- Horizon scanning
- Synthesizing ideas
- Writing reports
- Interviewing
- Persuading, influencing
- Writing
- Challenging others
- Managing conflict
- Being a team player

with those that you are really good at, and ending with those which you are not as good at.

Step 3

Next, using exactly the same list, write the capabilities down in the order that you like doing them.

For many people, the two lists will be in the same order, or very nearly so. And that's fine. But for some people, there are one or two capabilities which are at the top of one list and in a different place on the second list, maybe closer to the middle. This difference is useful: that's where the insight lies.

Step 4

Now put these capabilities on the worksheet at the end of this chapter, so that you can correlate the two lists. You can see on the worksheet where each list goes – along the top of the model is the list in ranked order of strength, and along the left-hand vertical axis is the list ranked in order of liking or enjoyment.

Step 5

Correlating the two lists is the key step: plot the point on the model where each capability meets in one of the four boxes of the model. That will tell you what kind of capability it is: natural strength, potential strength, fragile strength or resistant limitation.

Here's an example to show this more clearly.

CASE STUDY   Sara's potential strengths and resistant limitations

Sara is the operations and marketing manager in a small charity. She has a number of responsibilities, but one of her favourite tasks is co-ordinating the work of committed volunteers. They regularly contact her with suggestions for improvements and Sara enjoys these wide-ranging discussions, full of ideas and opinions. But Sara also has to synthesize their ideas into some workable proposals, and she feels she is not as good at this as she could be. Her analysis, using the Strengths model, suggested that this synthesizing skill is a *potential strength* – a skill that fits with the kind of person she is and which she could develop further into a natural strength. There may not be a specific training course for this, but she's seen the CEO of the organization do this well in meetings with community groups. By shadowing her in some key meetings, Sara hopes to learn more about how she might improve her own skill in this area.

As part of her management role, Sara also has to keep track of various operational and marketing budgets, and given that they are a charity, tight control is particularly vital. She's well aware of this, but the detailed numerical analysis of what's happening each month is not something she is very good at. It's a *resistant limitation* for her. She can't delegate this entirely because it's a key part of her responsibility,

FIGURE 7.4   Part of Sara's Strengths model

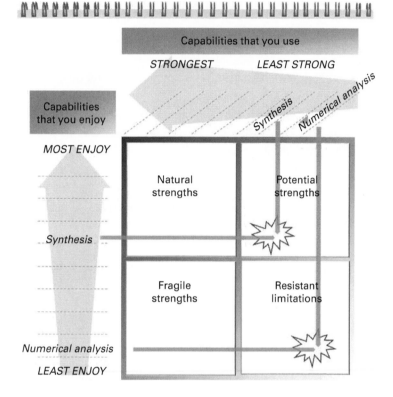

but this exercise gives her a possible solution. She could collaborate with a colleague who has a natural strength in setting up analytical spreadsheets and spotting the problems in the pattern of numbers. And, luckily, there is a new member of her team who is really good at this.

Her strategy is not to abdicate completely from the area of her resistant limitation, but rather to find someone who is expert in this area and genuinely work with them and listen to their advice.

EXTENSION IDEAS

- You might find it useful to consider how your various strengths have played out over time, throughout your working life. So look back at your Journey Map and consider your least rewarding or most demanding job: which of your capabilities did you have to use? Are they your natural strengths? Or, looking back, do you see that you were working with fragile strengths, or even with your resistant limitations? That might explain why that particular role was so hard.

- Have you developed a potential strength in the past? And, if so, how? Was it through formal training or self-study, or through working with a mentor or coach? Look back over the development activities you have done to see which kind has been most successful for you.

- Is there someone you could collaborate with now, who has a natural strength in the area where you have a resistant limitation? Although your strategy work isn't finished, it might be possible and useful to take action on this idea sooner rather than later.

- In taking on responsibility for your own development, you may find yourself having to explain your new approach and this model to your boss as part of a performance appraisal. This might be the only way to avoid being sent on yet another training course to address an area of 'weakness' in your performance. How will you do this? What can you prepare in advance of your performance appraisal discussion to help you explain your development plan to your boss?

SUMMARY

- Instead of assessing your capabilities as either strengths or weaknesses just on the basis of how good you are in each area, the Strengths model uses two dimensions: the first is how strong each capability is for you; and the second is whether your personality preferences help or hinder the exercise of that capability.

- There are three different types of strengths:
  - Natural strengths where your strong skill in this area fits with your psychometric preference – it's easy for you to be good at this area. Work *with* these strengths; they will fuel your success.
  - Potential strengths where your preferences suggest you should be good at this capability, but perhaps the strength isn't as good as it could be. Work *up* these areas because they are worth investing in and could become natural strengths.
  - Fragile strengths where your job requires a capability which doesn't fit with your preferences but which you have to do so often that you have become good at them. Work *on* these strengths, because they require constant effort to keep up.
- The final category is those capabilities in which you are not strong and they don't fit with the grain of your personality; these are not so much weaknesses that could be overcome as resistant limitations. Work *around* these, with strategies of collaboration – work with a colleague or team member who has a natural strength in the area which for you is a resistant limitation.
- This is a liberating idea because the model illustrates that it is psychologically impossible to be good at everything; the psychometric preferences that make you excellent in one area will make it difficult for you to be good in another area which requires the opposite characteristics. It also means that it's time to stop going on training courses to address a 'persistent weakness'. Try a different strategy to compensate for what you now know is a resistant limitation.

What's next?

If you have worked through all the chapters in Stage 2, you will have plenty of strategic insights: about what your ideal future might look like, what your purpose might be, and how you might go about developing your strengths. Now it's time to turn these insights into action – and that's what Stage 3 is about.

FIGURE 7.5 Strengths worksheet

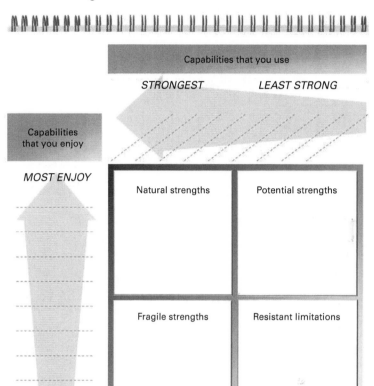

Making strategy real

Your strategy will make little difference to you unless you turn it into action. You could go so far as to say that the implementation work is more important than the strategizing itself. That's what this third and final stage of the book is about: taking some action and getting the next phase of your journey under way.

In Chapter 2, you prepared a map of the past, showing how you got to where you are now. Now, in Stage 3, we'll work on your map for the future. And the map metaphor is the right one, because the goal is not to create a perfectly detailed plan which you then simply implement. Your strategy is a statement of direction, and you'll need to adjust it from time to time. You should continue to think about your strategy even as you take action. But you won't want to set out on the journey without some preparations, and your implementation work will be easier with a plan or action list.

So the three chapters in this stage of the book blend both strategic thinking and tactical action planning. First, Chapter 8 will help you to think broadly about the career transitions you might want to make, with one final strategy model to help you. In Chapter 9, we will return to the Strategy Triangle to explore two different but complementary ways of implementing your strategy; this will help you to think about *what* you want to do and *how* you want to do it. Chapter 10 is about getting under way and actually taking the first few steps. It focuses on tactics – the specific, achievable steps that take you in the right direction. Tactics are more important than you might think because they give you the chance to adjust your strategy in a working world that changes all the time. And they still take you forward, as long as you can see where you are going.

CHAPTER EIGHT

Making a career transition

The Product/Market matrix

If you have come through the strategy process with a conviction that you want to make a change in your career, how will you go about doing that?

Why this matters to you

Making a new map for a better and more satisfying route to success almost always implies some change – and change often involves risk, especially since shifts in direction usually involve multiple adjustments. As we know from the Strategy Triangle, a change in one element – purpose, resources or opportunities – always implies some kind of change in the other two. This transition risk is particularly significant for women. Because women often have a whole range of other responsibilities to family and community, the risk can seem so large that such a move feels impossible to make. But this chapter has a useful and strategic perspective to offer about transitions and growth, both for organizations and for individuals. It will help you to see that a phased approach might be much more manageable as a way of getting to where you want to go.

Transition risk

There is a Monty Python comedy sketch set in a career adviser's office which is precisely about this kind of career transition. An accountant comes in for some advice; he says he wants a new job, something exciting that will let him live life to the full. He's decided he wants to be a lion tamer. The career counsellor comments that this seems a bit of a jump from accountancy. He suggests that it might be better to work his way step by step towards this ideal role, perhaps via a job in banking. But the candidate doesn't want to wait: he simply states that tomorrow morning at 9, he wants to be in there! The counsellor remarks that if he calls the circus now and offers the services of a 45-year-old accountant as a lion tamer, they are likely to ask what experience this candidate has with lions. It transpires that the candidate doesn't even know what a real lion is and has confused them with anteaters – different in scale, habitat and ferocity. It's a comedy sketch but, like many such sketches, it has a kernel of useful truth in it: you are likely to get hurt if you launch yourself into a career as a lion tamer with no knowledge at all of either lions or how to tame them.

There is actually a double risk here. One is getting the role in the first place, which is not always easy when employers want to manage their risk of hiring someone without any directly relevant experience. And then there is the risk in doing the role: even if you can get a completely different job in a new sector, it might prove hard to be successful in it, since you have so much to learn.

So one approach to this is the phased, pivot strategy – and that's where this model is useful. The accountant in the comedy sketch could take this approach, although that is not the point of the joke. He could, for example, take on an accounting role for a circus, get to know the people in the organization and take on the job of cleaning lion cages in the evening, to build up his knowledge of lions. And then he might be able to be a substitute assistant to the lion tamer from time to time. The very absurdity of the transition in the sketch could be managed; building up knowledge of the new context while still using existing skills is one place to start in making such a giant transition.

The idea

The idea in this chapter is to use the Product/Market matrix to help you plan your transition and manage the transition risk. The model is sometimes called the 'Product/Market Expansion

FIGURE 8.1 The Product/Market matrix

Grid' because it's about moving from your current position of selling your existing products in your existing markets into something new. The model does exactly what its title suggests: it gets you to think about what you have to sell and where you sell it. There is a parallel here between organizational growth and your individual career development. Think of your 'product' as what you have to offer, in terms of your capabilities and the work you can do, and the 'market' as the organizations which will employ you or pay you.

The diagram illustrates four basic approaches to organizational growth:

- **Market penetration:** Businesses can grow by focusing on their existing products and services in their existing markets to achieve greater market penetration. They might do this in various ways: making their prices more competitive, undertaking more sales and marketing activity, or designing and running product promotions or loyalty schemes to encourage existing customers to buy again. This is really about making small changes to current business operations – sharpening up business as usual.

- **Market development:** Where there is a need for more growth, businesses may seek to open new markets for their existing products. This might involve minor design or pricing changes, but the focus is on opening new markets and reaching new customers. The newness is what brings a higher level of risk, because if the organization doesn't really understand the new market, or what its customers want and will pay for, the investment may not result in business growth.

- **Product development:** Where a business seeks growth with a tolerable level of risk, managers may decide to develop new products for their existing markets. They draw on their existing knowledge of the market to do this, what they already know about their customers and their needs. They may also invest in some research and development work to generate some innovations in product design which they believe will be of interest to customers in this market.

- **Diversification:** This is the most risky approach – where an enterprise may decide to develop completely new products in order to launch them straightaway into new markets, tolerating the level of risk for the sake of a greater level of reward, and achieving it more quickly.

So, if the ultimate aim is to sell completely new products in a new market, the model shows three possible routes: two of them are incremental steps, and the third is a bold, innovative route to move into a new market with a new product all at once.

Using the model

This model can be useful to you in two ways. First, it can help you to generate ideas and options for developing your career, setting out some categories for your map. For example, one option might be to stay where you are and develop your skills further so that you can do more interesting work, or get promoted. You can see this in Figure 8.2, showing where you are now.

Second, if you are already clear about exactly where you want to get to, this model will help you to decide *how* best to do that. Are you going to change your 'product' first and then your 'market'? Or do you plan to change both at once?

If you want a completely different role in a different sector, you could simply start applying for such jobs. You might be successful, and then you'll have to work hard to become productive and successful in this completely new context. But that won't be easy and it carries some risk. It might even be almost impossible to get such a role without building some visibly relevant experience, so that you can move successfully from what you do now to what you want to do in the future. The Product/Market matrix usefully reminds us that there is more than one route to achieving that end goal; in particular, it shows that

FIGURE 8.2 Starting from your current position in the Product/Market matrix

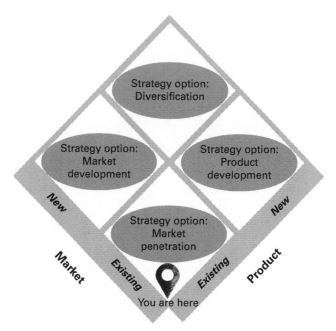

making the transition in a series of interim steps might be slower but it could be less risky and disruptive.

You might think of these interim steps as 'pivot strategies': either using your existing skills in a new organization, or developing new skills in your current organization. One part of your working life remains stable – either your role or your organization – and you 'pivot' from this stable base to make the change, either changing organization or role, but not both at the same time. This pivot strategy could be a key component of a plan for a major transition at work, as Millie's story in the case study shows.

CASE STUDY   Millie's path to self-employment

Everyone in Millie's family had always worked for big organizations, and so when she left university, she took a graduate trainee role in the IT department of a large company. It seemed the sensible thing to do. And she stayed with that organization throughout her twenties. But somewhere inside her lurked a completely different ambition: really, she wanted to work for herself, doing something more entrepreneurial. That's why she used the strategy exercises in this book – to try to resolve the conflict between the job she had taken and what she really wanted to do. Why had she chosen the option of working for a large organization? Because it seemed safe. A regular salary and a desk at head office. But she also realized that if she was going to change direction in her working life, it was probably now or never. There were risks, of course, but she felt that she simply had to face them.

So how was she going to move from employment in a large organization to self-employment? One obvious route was to become a contractor for her current employer. She would have to give up the team leadership role and learn to work as a freelancer, but she'd still be in the same organization, doing the same kind of work, maybe even at the same desk. Although this would reduce the risk, this option felt too tame to her – it didn't feel like she was making progress. So she used the Product/Market matrix to generate some other options.

The option she chose was to set herself up as a self-employed franchisee within a larger networked organization. She felt this would give her a safe introduction to self-employment. She signed up with a networked craft supplies business, which gave her both products as well as some structure and support from other franchise owners. Although she had known this business as a customer, it was essentially a new market for her skills – a new kind of context. Her existing skills in IT and administration were enough to get her started, but she needed the support from the franchise in areas where she didn't have expertise, such as accounting and sales. And gradually, over the next five years, she recruited a team of independent agents working with her, running creative craft workshops across her region and selling a wide range of art supplies.

Encouraged by her success, she set up a second business entirely on her own account, with no franchiser support. She looked at her capabilities to see what else she could use to build her own business and started group and individual language tuition, both from her own home and in commercial premises. Once again, she was moving into a new market, but this time she had already acquired the business

FIGURE 8.3 Millie's transition strategy

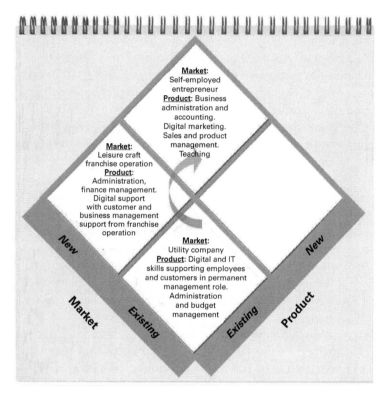

management skills she needed so the transition was less risky. She also noticed that she gained new customers for the craft business from those who signed up for her language classes. As a result, both businesses grew.

When the franchiser for her primary business suddenly withdrew from the UK market, she and her team were shocked. No one had expected that. But she now felt confident enough to be able to carry on both businesses on her own account, without that support.

Millie found that she could get where she wanted to go through a series of interim steps, and the Product/Market matrix helped her to plot her route from employment to entrepreneurship. This phased approach made the risk of that transition more manageable for her, both financially and in terms of workload.

Adele also took a phased approach to her career change, planning her route in a series of steps.

CASE STUDY Adele's search for her new role

Adele was itching for a change. She'd spent five years in the Learning and Development team in a financial services business and she was tired of being in a support role. She wanted to work in operations, actually dealing with customers. Not necessarily in the same sector, either – maybe in a consumer goods company, for example. But every time she had applied for operational jobs in other organizations, she had not even managed to get a first interview. She had plenty of experience in developing training material on regulatory requirements in financial services, but nothing directly relevant to a different sector, or to an operational role. And so she was never shortlisted and never had the chance to try to persuade a potential new employer that she was worth employing.

The Product/Market matrix exercise gave her a new approach. Her first step was to make a move within her current organization, volunteering to join a project to work with operational team leaders developing the training required for the implementation of a new system. This first step was about using her existing 'product' – the ability to develop training programmes – in a new and different part of her current organization in order to build her knowledge of operational departments. Once she had developed the training material, she then began to work with the operational managers to deliver the training. She got to know the operational team leaders and they got to know her – and so when an operational role was advertised in that same department, they were more than willing to consider her application. For them, there was an obvious risk in taking on someone with no previous operational experience, but they agreed to a secondment from the L&D department for six months because she had proved that she could learn fast. Adele was delighted, and at the end of the six months, her secondment was made permanent. She still aimed at a more senior operational role in another industry sector to broaden her CV, but she was now much better placed to make successful job applications.

FIGURE 8.4 Adele's transition strategy

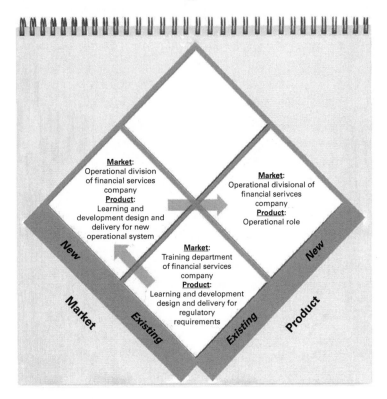

Figure 8.4 shows Adele's analysis.

Using this approach, Adele found a new route to get where she wanted to go. The two interim steps might be a slower route, but she was at least making some progress.

Parallels with corporate strategy

Organizations use the Product/Market matrix to assess the viability and risk of possible new initiatives, and to help articulate a range of possible scenarios in the search for growth. The model turns the more complex and mathematical Ansoff matrix – which we will look at next – into a simple framework to consider strategic options. Once again, it's a model that is useful in formulating strategy, but it also helps with implementation planning. It forces an enterprise to be clear about exactly how and when to grow from its current position, moving from selling its existing products in its existing markets to something new. Those implementation decisions are important, since the implications of taking one route or another can be very significant for the organization, both financially and in terms of reputation.

The parallel with corporate strategy for individuals is that we, too, want to grow and develop, maybe get promoted, take on increasing levels of responsibility, or change direction. Using this model will help you to think clearly about possible options for you. In exactly the same way that an organization might plan to open a new market for its existing products, you might choose to take a 'market development' approach to your career. If you decide to take on a similar kind of role, using your existing skills but in a new sector, you'll probably need to trade on your reputation and experience to get as far as the interview. And once appointed, you'll have to allow yourself some time to learn about your new context – new organization, new sector – in order to be successful. But with this approach, you are only changing one thing at a time and you have your existing capabilities to rely on.

Your strategy work so far might have shown you that you need to develop some of your skills – in other words, to take a product development approach. And if you still want to stay in the same organization, you'll want to be sure that your 'market' recognizes your new skills and the value of them. But if your strategy work tells you that what you need is a very different working life – a completely new role, in a different organization – you might want to manage the risk of making so large a transition in a single step. That's not to say you shouldn't contemplate that – after all, we have only so much time in life – but the Product/Market matrix offers you some alternative approaches.

The underlying research

The Ansoff matrix was developed in the 1950s and has been widely used in all sorts of sectors to help identify strategic options for growth. Igor Ansoff was a mathematician, and his matrix focuses on two key dimensions: products and markets (Ansoff, 1957). Each of those two dimensions can be further split into groups, making the simple two-by-two matrix richer and more complicated. Products can be described as existing, or modified, or completely new, and markets can be defined either by geography (same or different) or by target customer group (current or new).

As many strategists note, the matrix worked well in the conditions in which it was developed but its focus on two particular dimensions – products and markets – ignores other dimensions of strategy which have since become very significant. For example, the Ansoff matrix omits the dimension of competitor activity. In the 21st century, the market disruption caused by a competitor action (for example, in developing a completely new product which alters an existing market) is too significant to be ignored. In corporate terms, you just have to think about the development of the digital camera, which has all but wiped out the market for traditional film cameras and films themselves, although there are still pockets of the professional market where these products are valued. Then consider the inclusion of a camera in most mobile phones, which has changed the way most customers buy these items.

The application to you

In applying this idea to individual careers, we don't think so much about competition, but more about the disruption in the job market that comes from innovation. There are obvious examples of digital and internet developments changing the nature of some jobs, or even destroying them. Consider insurance brokers and travel agents: the information aggregation and advice that they used to provide and which we used to pay for is now obtainable for free from the web and from crowdsourced reviews. Both jobs still exist, but their customer base and services are now rather different. There is more disruption ahead from a whole range of causes: the development of artificial intelligence or recessionary pressures are just two examples. Working lives will change and new roles arise as others simply disappear.

That's part of the reason why having your own strategy is so important; although you might want to make some changes in what you do, it is also very likely that external forces will require you to make changes in one way or another. To use the language of this chapter, markets will change, and if we want or need to keep working, we will have to change too.

And there are various ways of making these changes. Some will suit you and some not. Some will work better for you at this stage of your life than others. To help you think about the choices you might make, here are three examples of women who have made changes in their working lives in different ways. First, Maria: she has learned to take risks in making big career changes, diversifying straight into new organizations and rapidly developing new skills.

CASE STUDY Maria's diversification approach

Maria has a corporate career which has taken her from Canada to Europe and then to the US. Her career map shows some definite changes of direction, but she's managed those transitions by taking carefully calculated risks. At each point, she's assessed carefully what would be asked of her in the new role and has decided for herself whether she could actually deliver it. She tells this as a story of the benefit of seizing the unexpected opportunity, but simultaneously analysing carefully what will make it a success.

In the last year of her degree in psychology, she started looking for jobs in journalism. Despite a number of rejections from magazines, she tried writing directly to an international magazine, asking for work. To her surprise, they took her on on a short-term contract. Then, they asked her to stay on permanently. She was stunned, but delighted. She felt that maybe she could 'punch above her weight' – that despite the lack of relevant experience on her CV, her attitude and focus could help her to achieve.

Her next job was a corporate role in a completely new field, so in the first few months she focused on learning as much as she could, as fast as possible. She drew on her earlier experience of 'not being afraid to raise my hand, to respond to a challenge'. She discovered that she could learn quickly enough to take on something new, provided that she was clear with he new employer about what would be needed for her to make the transition. Once again, she used her analytical skills to define in advance what she would need from them as well as what she could deliver and when.

Later in her corporate career, a former colleague called her, asking her to take on a role as head of HR and communications, based in Brussels. Maria was surprised to be considered for this – she told her former colleague bluntly, 'I have no experience in HR and I know nothing about Europe.' This open and honest approach has proved successful for her. She talks about the overt assessment she does of these opportunities with each potential new boss: 'I want to be sure that what you *think* I can deliver, I *know* I can deliver.' She has learned to blend careful scrutiny of what's required in each role and open discussion with her employers to fuel her courage to rise to each new challenge.

In the next example, Caroline takes a different approach, using her volunteer work running alongside her paid work to help her pivot into a new role. This parallel running is often seen in organizational contexts and it can work well for individuals too, in some phases of life.

CASE STUDY   Caroline's pivot strategy: the benefits of volunteering

Caroline has had a varied corporate career, with roles in HR, communications and PR, and has also worked as an entrepreneur setting up and running owner-managed businesses in fields very different from her corporate expertise.

She achieves these moves into different fields through a conscious strategy of volunteering as a means of learning, as well as of contributing to the organization for which she volunteers. This is her version of a pivot strategy. She serves in unpaid roles, in parallel with her paid employment, both to gain experience and to help build a network of contacts in the field. Her advice is to 'volunteer where you can watch and learn from others, so that you are able to give but also to get simultaneously'. Her strategy requires considerable investment of time and energy to manage both her volunteer role and her job, so she also recommends 'choosing to volunteer in something that's important to you because that will help to keep you motivated'.

Her work as a volunteer in various capacities throughout her career has given her new experience and has helped her change direction, through what she has learned as well as through the increase in confidence that comes from learning to work in a new field.

Patricia used the Product/Market matrix as part of her reflection on her career to date, to help her to think differently about her experience and the expertise she had developed from it.

CASE STUDY   Patricia's transition experience

Patricia's CV shows that she has moved between private sector organizations and public sector bodies several times in her career. Her first job was in a private sector company working with public sector clients both in the UK and abroad; her second role was in a public sector organization – a university research team – working in partnership with a single private sector organization to solve a particular problem. Her working life has been full of variety as a result, but she had never previously consciously thought about exactly how she had managed to make those transitions.

When Patricia prepared her own Journey Map, a visual representation of the various jobs she had done in her working life so far, she could see just how many times she had moved from one sector to another. And she could see that, mostly, those moves had gone well; she had stayed in each new post for a number of years and had been promoted, too. So maybe her adaptability was a real skill. That insight encouraged her to include this evidence in her application letters for new roles, as a way of showing potential employers that the risk of appointing her to a new role in a new organization was much less than they might think. And it also felt less risky for her to make such transitions – she felt bolder when she reflected on what she had done in the past to adapt to new contexts.

Using this model as a way to re-examine your working life to date can be interesting and productive. It might be helpful in recasting your Journey Map, providing another perspective, as it was for Patricia. But at this point in your strategy work, we'll focus on using the model as a different way of thinking about your future and your possible next steps, and that's what the exercise below will help you with.

The exercise: guidance

In using this model, the idea is to populate each quadrant so that you can see your various options for career growth and how you might achieve them. The exercise allows you to explore four different scenarios for your future career and to think about how you might move from one to the next. As you do this, you may find that you just don't know enough about these options, and that will help you to do some market research at an early stage in your planning. The worksheet at the end of this chapter will help you to keep track of your thinking.

Step 1

Start with your current position: what you are selling now and where. In other words, describe your current capabilities and the work you do as if it were a product being sold to the existing market of your current employer, or the organization which pays you for your work. To do this, use the following questions:

- What is your 'market' – your employer or the organization which pays you? And who are the 'customers' you serve? This might include internal colleagues or external members of the public.

- What is your 'product' – what outcomes do you produce for those customers? What capabilities do you use in doing this?

Capture these ideas in the bottom quadrant.

Step 2

Staying in this quadrant, think about a strategy of 'market penetration'. In an individual context, this might be about internal promotion, applying for a new role, or raising your profile to demonstrate more clearly your existing capabilities. Here are some questions to help you consider your options:

- Are there more senior roles in your current department which you aspire to?
- What do the job advertisements for these roles list as requirements?
- Are there internal promotion processes in your organization and are you well placed for them?
- What could you do to demonstrate your capabilities and be of more value to the organization? For example, could you volunteer for a company-wide project or join a mentoring scheme?

Step 3

Now think about a strategy of 'product development'. In Chapter 7, on your strengths, you may have already identified that there are some capabilities which you could usefully develop. If you did this, how could you use them in your current role and organization? How would they be useful to your 'market'? Capture your ideas in the right-hand quadrant of the worksheet.

Step 4

Next, consider a scenario in which you move to a different organization – or to a different part of your current organization – but in the same kind of role. This is a strategy of 'market development' – the left-hand quadrant of the worksheet. You might need to do some market research to explore this idea.

- Which other organizations might offer you the kind of role you have now?

- What are they like? Large or small, public or private sector, hierarchical or loosely structured, with employees or freelance associates, located in one place or spread geographically across the country?

- Have these organizations recruited people from outside into roles like yours before? Or are these roles really only accessible to internal candidates?

Describe this scenario in the left-hand quadrant of the worksheet.

Step 5

Now explore the option where you make a complete change of direction in your career, taking on a new role, in a different type of organization. This is what is called a strategy of diversification in this model. In the top quadrant of the model, describe the 'market' – the ideal type of organization you want to work for. Describe the role you want as the new 'product' you want to be able to offer, in terms of capabilities required and the things you would do in that role. To develop your thinking, here are some questions you might try to answer:

- Look at job advertisements for your ideal job in this new organization or sector. What sort of experience do they require?

- Using your network, find someone who actually does your ideal role now. How did they get the job? What do they like about their job or dislike about it?

- What would be the risk of moving to such a new role in a new organization immediately – for you and for your potential new employer?

- What interim steps could you take to get to this new role in a series of pivots?

Step 6

At the end of this exercise, you'll have a clearer picture of the possible options open to you. Now you have to make a choice: will you pivot through some interim roles to help you get a completely different role? Or do you just want to grow in your existing market context? There is no right or wrong answer and your instinct will tell you whether any one of these scenarios appeals more than others. And that's the basis for your implementation plan.

EXTENSION IDEAS

- For 'market development' ideas, using your existing skills, explore the idea of adjacent sectors. What kinds of organizations have people in similar roles to yours but operate in slightly different sectors? For example, private and public sector providers which offer similar kinds of roles. Assemble a list of similar organizations, and ask yourself whether one of these might be worth researching in more detail. For example, if you work for a housing association, is there is council or government department which provides similar types of service? Or if you work for a retailer, are there technology firms which have similar customers and which market or sell their products in similar ways?

- If you are contemplating a 'product development' approach, planning to invest in developing your capabilities so that you can do more and different things, look back at the Strengths model in Chapter 7. Will it be easy or hard for you to develop in these areas? Does the answer change your view of your strategy for making a career change?

SUMMARY

- The Product/Market matrix helps organizations to think about possible routes for growth. The simplified version of Ansoff's multidimensional matrix sets out a range of options for selling existing or new products in a current or new market.

- It does the same for individuals if we think of our capabilities and what we do at work as the 'product' and the employer or paying organization as the 'market'.

- The model helps to articulate what development may be required to implement your new strategy, through four possible routes for growth:

  - **Market penetration:** selling existing products to expand the current market;

  - **Market development:** developing new markets for existing products;

  - **Product development:** developing new products for an existing market;

  - **Diversification:** developing new products for a new market.

- The four possible options carry different levels of risk in career terms. This is particularly relevant for women since the multiple roles and varied responsibilities which women tend to carry can sometimes constrain their ability to make a career change, perhaps because they can't risk the loss or reduction of income, or they may have less freedom to move geographically.

- But the options also operate as interim steps, to allow you to plan a more gradual transition route from where you are now to where you want to be. That can be a useful way of managing the risk and be a framework for implementing your new career strategy.

FIGURE 8.5 Product/Market worksheet

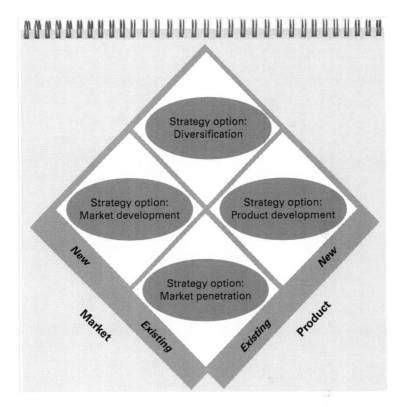

What's next?

Now that you have done so much thinking and research, it's time to turn your attention to action. The next chapter will help you to implement your strategy for the next phase of your working life. Whichever route you've chosen from the exercise in this chapter, you'll want to make an action plan for what you will actually do when you finish this book.

CHAPTER NINE

Turning your new strategy into action: planning and experimenting

Now that you have assembled a range of insights and ideas about your ideal future, how will you make this real? How will you implement your strategy?

Why this matters to you

At the end of residential programmes at the University of Oxford, we reach what we call the 'So what?' stage. This is where we ask programme participants to think specifically about how they will implement the insights they have had during the programme and what's next for them.

This chapter poses the same question to you: what are you actually going to *do*? Strategy is important, but implementation is what counts. And it would be very odd to have a book about success strategies which simply didn't cover the topic of implementation.

Making your own map is useful, vital even, but if it doesn't guide your decisions and choices, it's not going to help you as much as it could.

The obvious answer is that you now need some kind of plan. It doesn't necessarily have to be the traditional kind of plan, just some kind of preparatory process that works for you. You have some choices here, and this chapter describes them.

The idea

In a complex and rapidly changing world, the idea of a career plan can feel rigid and old fashioned. That is why this book focuses on strategy and strategic direction: because you need a sense of direction as well as the ability to respond to what happens in the outside world. As famous Prussian military commander Helmuth von Moltke said, 'No plan of operations reaches with any certainty beyond the first encounter with the enemy's main force.' The business version of that might be that no business plan survives first contact with customers.

But this doesn't imply that planning is unnecessary. Organizations know that the process of planning is probably more important than the resulting plan. It's somewhat surprising that many of us don't spend time planning for our own working lives, given how much time we spend working on our employer's business plans, budgets and forecasts. But we often don't apply that expertise to ourselves, preferring to improvise our way through our careers, with loose assumptions about what we want and how to achieve it (Golzen and Garner, 1990). Successful strategy implementation hinges on planning: thinking ahead, defining the next steps and scheduling them. But you also have to be ready to adapt your plans to take account of the realities of the job market and the changes in your life. In other words, planning is necessary, but not by itself sufficient; your ability to stay connected to the external world and responsive to it is also vital.

Two different implementation approaches

When you think about the approach you want to take to implementing your strategy, the Strategy Triangle is helpful, just as it was in formulating your strategy. It illustrates two different approaches you might take to implementation.

So far, in the exercises in this book, you've been focusing on the three elements of the Strategy Triangle, one at each point: purpose, resources (such as your capabilities, skills and knowledge) and opportunities. But now look at the left- and right-hand *sides* of the triangle, running from the base to the apex. One side of the triangle focuses on internal organization and the development of your resources in line with your purpose. Your strategy work will have given you more insight about your strengths and skills, and you now also have a clearer articulation of your purpose. If you are contemplating self-development as a key action in your plan, you'll obviously want that to be in line with your purpose statement. And in these two areas, you have a degree of control and of self-knowledge, so a structured plan of some kind will help you to take action.

The other side of the triangle focuses externally, on opportunities, particularly those that are in line with your purpose. Here, you have much less control over the opportunities which are out

FIGURE 9.1 The Strategy Triangle

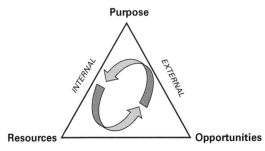

Adapted from Professor Marcus Alexander's Strategy Triangle.

there, or which might arise in the next few months. You probably also have much less knowledge of them. Your possible next steps might not be as clear you'd like: you may feel unsure about the route to get you where you want to go. Or you might even be doubtful about your eventual destination. Is there really an opportunity for the kind of successful work you are looking for? This kind of uncertainty about either your route or your end goal is not something to worry about. Rather, it suggests that you need a different implementation approach: a more experimental exploration of different possibilities.

The blend of these two approaches is the key idea in successful implementation of your strategy. You will need some kind of plan but you also need to remain open to the unexpected opportunity that comes along. Too rigid a plan might make you miss an interesting career chance – but, equally, having no plan at all might well prevent you from getting to where you want to go. The trick is to keep these two approaches in balance. Corporate strategists recommend this blend of planning and opportunism (Williamson, 1999), and it applies to individuals, too.

How do you find the ideal blend? Here's one simple way: assess how well you understand your possible next steps. Where it's clear to you what you might do next, develop a plan and a schedule. For those areas where you are not clear, deliberately take a more experimental, exploratory approach. For example, if you know you want to apply for a leadership role in your current organization, develop a schedule for yourself of performance review times and promotion requirements. If, on the other hand, you think you might be interested in a job-share opportunity, but you don't really understand how such an arrangement could work, try a series of small experiments. You might start by taking on a shared role outside work in a voluntary organization or community group to see if this way of working will suit you.

In the example below, Joanna uses both approaches – the planned and the opportunistic – when things suddenly change at work.

CASE STUDY   Joanna's next steps

Joanna works for an investment management company and has recently managed to make the move from a back-office role to one of the trading teams. She and a colleague were appointed on secondment to two temporary junior analyst roles for six months; Joanna has relished the move because it was always part of her strategy to work in the front office. She likes her colleagues and is learning from them, and she is starting to study for her professional exams. She gave herself a pat on the back for getting this job so early in her career.

But now the situation has changed. Although everyone expected that these secondments would turn into permanent roles, budget pressures now mean that's unlikely. In fact, there is only one permanent role and she and her colleague will have to compete for it, along with anyone else who wants to apply. Joanna feels like the rug has been pulled out from under her feet. She thought she had achieved one of her strategic goals, but now it looks like she needs a new plan.

The first phase of her new plan is research: she needs to find out more about the process and timetable for this appointment. Will it be a formal interview process, and, if so, how can she draw on the experiences of the last six months to strengthen her case? What will happen if she doesn't get the permanent role? Will she return to the back-office role or is there another option? She's not entirely happy about how things will work out, and feels it might help her confidence to know what other similar roles are available elsewhere, and what the recruitment market is like right now. So she does two things: she arranges to have a coffee with a recruitment consultant one evening after work, just to see what opportunities there might be, and she signs up for an online industry conference with other organizations in the sector. These experiments might help her to see other ways of getting where she wants to go.

She realizes that there's another priority for her: it would be useful to have a performance appraisal before the interview process starts. So she plans to set up a meeting with her boss and starts to draft her own self-appraisal to use in the discussion.

Joanna's response to the sudden change in circumstances is to do some planning to prepare for the interview, but also to explore what might be on offer in other organizations, just as an experiment. The combination of the two approaches gives her some focus for the next few weeks in implementing her new plan, and a sense of confidence that there might be other opportunities externally if the interview doesn't go as well as she hopes.

Devising your implementation approach

Devising the right implementation approach for your strategy hinges on two decisions: *what* to do and *how* to do it. Are you clear about what needs to be changed – clear enough to devise a simple plan for yourself? Or are there new ideas and options bubbling up which still need to be explored? If so, you might need a phase of experimentation to clarify whether they are realistic.

WHAT TO DO

Let's start by looking at what you feel you need to do. If you have done any of the exercises in Stage 2, where you look at your future options, you will have a list of things you want to change. But is it the right list? Is it complete? Are your next steps clear to you?

If you're trying to make a change in your working life, there will usually be a cluster of related alterations. Take an obvious example: if you want a new qualification and have signed up to a development programme, you will probably have to alter your schedules and renegotiate some commitments, just to make the time to do the programme. In the same way, making a major career shift also requires a series of alterations if it is to be successful and sustainable. The first task in devising your implementation strategy is to think through all the changes you want to make and in what order you want to make them.

The exercise in Chapter 6, the Purpose Alignment model, is about this logical interconnection between parts of your life.

The point of this model is that the stronger the logical alignment between all the various things we do and our purpose, the more successful we are likely to be and the more satisfied we will probably feel. It's also about getting the support mechanisms right, too, or logically aligned. Although this is a key strategic idea, it's also the idea expressed in various poems and proverbs, including in some words from Benjamin Franklin: 'For want of a nail the shoe was lost, for want of a shoe the horse was lost; and for want of a horse the rider was lost; being overtaken and slain by the enemy, all for want of care about a horse-shoe nail.' This story is often interpreted as being about mistakes or omissions, but it's really about the interconnectedness of things, and how success might depend on a chain of apparently minor actions. Sometimes a small and specific change can be key in making a more significant set of changes.

All good planning contains a mix of actions: large-scale strategic actions plus the smaller tactical steps which are logically necessary to achieve the end goal. The big strategic decisions are probably clearer to you now. But there is always a set of little decisions that you make every day, maybe unconsciously, which are also still strategic in their impact. Can you see this mix as you define your list of what you need to do?

When you start your list of what you want to do, there will be some obvious actions and some obvious next steps. But there might also be some things on your list that are still vague. You may still be uncertain about what precisely to do next, even after all the thinking and reflection that you've done. Or maybe you have a nagging feeling that there might be a better option for you out there, if only you knew what it was. The lack of clarity is not necessarily a problem; it just suggests a different approach to implementation.

HOW TO DO IT
After thinking about what you want to do, take a moment to make a conscious decision about exactly how you want to do it.

Your choice of approach depends to a great extent on whether you can see an obvious action or not. But it also partly depends on your own preferences: maybe you are someone who likes structure and the idea of a proper implementation plan appeals to you. Or maybe you're an opportunity-focused person who likes to explore and experiment. Whatever your situation, the chances are that you will need to try both approaches, unless you have a very short list of completely clear actions. And don't worry if you find that you still aren't completely certain about everything, despite all your effort: it's wise not to be too definite about your planned actions in an essentially uncertain world. One of my favourite quotations about careers is a particularly vivid version of this same point: 'There's no such thing as a career path: it is crazy paving and you have to lay it yourself' (Sir Dominic Cadbury, cited in Mann, 2004). So with the benefit of all the insights you have gathered during this strategy process, you can start to think about the 'crazy paving stones' you have to work with and how you want to lay them.

In the rest of this section, we look in more detail at each of these two main approaches to making your strategy real so that you can devise the ideal blend for you.

Planning: five useful ideas

Planning is almost always a key part of your implementation approach. But there are various choices about the kind of plan you might develop. You might want a Gantt chart with dates and targets on it. Maybe you'd prefer just to annotate your calendar, or perhaps you are an aficionado of the bullet journal approach to planning. You might try writing yourself a set of instructions for how to get from Step 1 to 2 to 3 and beyond. But you will need something: just having the aspiration by itself is almost never enough.

This chapter is not intended to be a basic primer on how to draw up a plan, but rather to encourage you to include in your planning five particular characteristics which – because you are planning for yourself as an individual – will help you to make your plan more implementable. To make these five ideas more memorable, they all begin with letter P – let's call them the Five Ps of personal planning.

Priorities are obviously important, and there are several different types. The most obvious are those things that must be done first in sequence, so that later tasks can build on that work. But your list of priorities should also include those things that are simply the most important and must get done first, in case you don't have time, energy or inclination to implement the rest of the plan. And, of course, there are the 'quick wins' – the small and relatively easy changes which aren't really the most important save that they will give you a sense of progress and achievement. Developing a set of priorities makes the planning work easier, although it's not always easy to develop a short list. Sometimes everything feels like a priority and that can be overwhelming and confusing: where is the best place to get started?

Posteriorities are worth thinking about in those circumstances – and that's the second P. These are defined by Peter Drucker as 'opportunities or commitments which offer little or no significant long-term value to our lives. There are options we must teach ourselves to say no to in order to conserve energy, time and concentration for our true priorities' (Drucker, 2002). Although this sounds simple, it's quite hard to decide what to say no to, because what may be one of your posteriorities is almost always someone else's priority – and it's usually a person you work with closely! But when you are drawing up your list of actions, identify those things which you might like to get done but you could sacrifice if you had to. This will help you to avoid creating a plan which feels too demanding to implement.

Phases will be important in your plan for the future, just as they have been in your career so far. You will have seen in the Journey Map you prepared in Chapter 2 that there were a series of different phases in your life, perhaps when you started work or took on your first management or team supervisor role. As you prepare your plan, one simple idea is to break the year ahead into manageable blocks with a theme or target attached to each one. For example, there will be a phase of getting started, or researching options; maybe there will be an internally focused phase of reorganizing things within your team, or even a phase when you don't make much progress - say, over a holiday. Planning for those phases will mean that your schedule is more realistic and will feel more achievable.

Pauses are worth building into your plan – points where you will take a breath and review how it's going. I usually put a pause into any plan I make, particularly when taking on a new job. That's the first point at which I will ask myself whether the new job is working, and not before. If you review your plans too early, you run the risk of basing your review too much on gut feeling. For example, people sometimes say that you can't really tell whether you like your new job until you have been there at least three months. So if someone asks you whether things are going well in the first week of the new job, your answer is likely to be yes, because you are still in the honeymoon phase. The right answer is: ask me again in 12 weeks. The same is true for the new approaches you may be taking to your working life. Planning in a pause for reflection will allow you to check whether you are still going in the right direction.

Prizes is code for rewards – I had to have a word that begins with P to make all five ideas memorable! Building in a small reward for yourself at certain points helps motivation and serves as a good milestone showing how far you have come. You can plan in a reward which brings some other benefits, too: maybe after a day with friends at a health spa, you'll return to your plan with a new infusion of energy. It can be something small, maybe unrelated to your plan, but it marks a particular milestone and fosters a sense of achievement which will fuel you for the next stage.

Experimenting and exploring

The other way of implementing your strategy is to take an experimental, opportunistic approach. Sometimes, people feel that the word 'opportunistic' comes with some negative connotations, suggesting that you are simply drifting along seizing whatever random opportunities arise. But if you have a strategy, that won't be true for you. If you have done even a few of the exercises in this book, your insights will help you to make better choices about which opportunities to take up and which to ignore. Opportunism in line with your strategy, in other words.

In reality, this experimental approach is almost always useful whatever your situation. However you choose to implement your strategy, leave yourself time to notice and to explore. You don't want to miss a new and interesting opportunity which suddenly arises because you are too focused on the deadlines in your implementation plan. Even if you are clear about your destination and the route you want to take, this experimental approach will help you stay open to new ideas and spot changes in the organizations you'd like to work for, or the work you want to do, which might turn into opportunities. So here's the suggestion: as part of your strategy implementation, challenge yourself to run some small, regular career experiments. For example, you might decide every other month to go to a networking meeting in an industry that you don't know well or to attend a seminar on a topic that interests you but is not in your area of expertise. Alternatively, you might want to construct a deliberate, focused experiment to see whether you really do have a clear idea of the destination you seek, the job that will be ideal for you. When you decide to take this exploratory approach, it's as well to remember that good experiments don't just succeed or fail; they give you information, you learn from them and they help you to test hypotheses, but only if you know why you are exploring this idea and what assumptions you want to test.

There is one other reason why you might want to allow yourself some time to try things out. Many books about career success talk about 'finding your passion', but sometimes we only find what we are passionate about when we try something, take some action, experiment. Sometimes the end goal becomes clear only through actual experience. This might be a perfectly viable approach at certain times in your life, when you have time and energy to explore something new, and can afford to take a risk. It might not feel so comfortable if you are the breadwinner and also need to be home each night at 5.30 to feed the family. But even then don't dismiss the idea of experimentation: running a small, easy trial to see if you can make something work for you may help you formulate your new map.

Here's an example of a woman who deliberately planned a phase of experimentation to help her clarify what kind of work she was looking for, and to test her ideas.

CASE STUDY   Michelle's phase of experiments

Michelle is a doctor specializing in paediatrics who runs a children's clinic in a large university hospital. She describes her purpose as 'improving the medical care of as many children as possible' and her work in the clinic is absolutely in line with it.

Over the last few years, she has taken three weeks off each year to volunteer in Africa, setting up and running temporary clinics for children in remote areas. Her interest in field medicine is growing and she wonders whether she might make this her main role. But she's not quite sure exactly how this might be achieved, or whether it really is the right destination for her. There's a funding issue: the organizations she volunteers with have funding only for policy roles – temporary assignments to work with the World Health Organization (WHO). Would a policy role allow her to make more of a difference? Or would she rather continue to volunteer in local clinics for a few weeks each year? Or is there a different option for her to develop her interest in field medicine while still paying the rent? It's hard for her to make a plan with such unanswered questions.

After some thought, she decides on a deliberate programme of experimentation over the next year, to see what she learns, while still doing her full-time role at the hospital. To be specific, she decides she needs to attend a week's seminar on medical policymaking to see if this is really what she wants to do; she sets up some conversations over coffee with doctors who have moved into the policy area for WHO, to ask them about their work; and she volunteers to work as an adviser to a regional body looking at children's medical provision in her own country.

She's given herself a year as a first phase of her strategy implementation. These new 'test-and-learn' activities, running alongside her existing work, will allow her to experiment to see how best to realize her purpose. Then, she can plan her next phase with greater clarity.

Michelle has found an alternative option for living out her purpose and her experiments are designed to help her clarify whether it is a realistic one.

Here's a second example of a woman who was not at all clear about her ideal destination. She started off her strategy work with an experiment, because making her new map proved impossible without a clearer idea of what kind of thing she wanted to do. For her, experimentation was a way of uncovering her purpose.

CASE STUDY   Rosie's experiments

Rosie was feeling stuck. Her current job at a retailer bored her, and after four years in the role, she felt there was nothing more she could learn. But she didn't have an alternative. What did she want to do next? And what was she qualified for? She'd had a variety of jobs in different companies, trade associations and local government, and she could turn her hand to a range of roles. But she wasn't expert in any one area. 'I'm a bit of a generalist' was her own description. So, even if she did identify the perfect job, how would she persuade a potential employer that she had something useful to contribute?

As she began her strategy work, she realized that one of her strengths was precisely this ability to take on a wide variety of jobs, running projects, dealing with administrative details and also helping colleagues. Would her general skills be enough to build the rest of her working life on? She had no idea, so decided to run an experiment. She got a job as general assistant to the director of the local leisure centre and found that the role really did involve a wide range of different duties. One morning she would be taking minutes for the management committee and the next she had to organize contract cleaners. Occasionally she had to help with fundraising – and she quickly realized that this was not the job for her!

Then, during the winter, when things were quieter, she went to shadow one of the sports coaches, who worked with groups from local schools. She said this was a revelation for her. 'I loved the energy and enthusiasm of the children and could see that these sessions made a real difference to them. What a great way to spend the working day!' This gave her a new start for her strategy work: she now knew that she wanted to work with children and young people. But she still had to make a map to get into that field so she turned to the Product/Market exercise to see how she could use her existing skills to make that move.

For Rosie, the experimentation of taking the job at the leisure centre was a way of uncovering her purpose. She wasn't clear about her ideal job at this point in her life, and therefore couldn't begin to make a plan, or even to see what a useful next step might be. But by deliberately taking a job with a varied set of duties, she could explore some new options. Some of them she ruled out immediately, but one of them became her new destination.

Parallels with corporate strategy

In the 21st-century corporate world, some organizations feel that the traditional strategic planning approaches are too slow to be effective in rapidly changing circumstances. Instead, they develop what academics call an 'emergent' strategy, one which proceeds through some carefully considered, controlled experiments. These organizations focus strongly on the external dimension of the

Strategy Triangle. Alternatively, other organizations take a short-term, internal focus in very turbulent times. For example, during the UK's Brexit discussions in 2018, some British organizations decided that their best strategic approach was simply to concentrate on their processes and people, rather than speculate about future scenarios, so that they would be ready to respond quickly when the outcome of the Brexit negotiations became clearer. Their objective was to build resilience and flexibility: resilience in their leaders to manage through the uncertainty and flexibility in the organization to be able to replan, restructure and reallocate resources quickly and efficiently to respond to whatever might happen.

The blend of these two approaches to implementation in corporate strategy is sometimes referred to as strategic opportunism. This has been defined as 'the ability to remain focused on long-term objectives while staying flexible enough to solve day-to-day problems and recognize new opportunities' (Isenberg, 1987). In this context, the strategy sets out a general direction, while organizational leaders scan for and seize opportunities that arise – exactly as in the Strategy Triangle. And because strategizing is an iterative process, sometimes exploring the opportunity results in a change in strategic direction. Then something else may need to shift to keep the Strategy Triangle in balance. And so on.

Implementation can feel like a particularly messy part of strategy. It's an iterative process, which mixes up strategy and tactics, focusing on the short-term actions and the long-term goals, on today's operations as well as tomorrow's strategic choices. And the implementation work often feeds the development of a new strategy because of what was learned from what was done. So, although this book focuses first on strategy formulation and then on implementation, in reality they are intermingled. You may well find yourself iterating between thinking about strategy and taking some actions and then looping back to rethink and try a different approach. Don't be discouraged if that's what you find: it's not because you are not doing the strategizing work properly. Quite the reverse: you are staying open to the changes around you which might blow you off course, or open up a whole new route to a new destination. In the example above, you'll have seen that Rosie deliberately planned an experiment before starting her strategy work, because she simply didn't know enough about what she might want to do. So sometimes taking action in advance of your thinking will help you. For example, you'll have seen that some of the extension ideas in each chapter are really opportunities to take some action early, even before you have finished your thinking. This blend of thought and action can often be exactly the right approach, as we'll discuss in the last chapter.

The underlying research

Research on the factors which affect careers and their trajectories identifies two categories: personal determinants and situational determinants (Super, 1980). These two categories underline the usefulness of blending these two implementation approaches: the planned and the experimental.

Personal determinants are defined as those aspects of yourself which affect the way you think about your career and the choices you make. They include your values, attitudes and belief systems, as well as your skills and aptitudes. You may be conscious or unconscious of them, but the reflective strategy work you have done in the course of this book will have uncovered some of them. And although many of these determinants won't change, because they are part of who you are, some might alter. For example, you can develop new skills, as we covered in the Strengths model in Chapter 7. You might cultivate a new interest at a particular stage in your life, or you might suddenly realize that it's time to turn one of your childhood passions into paid work, now, before it's too late. That's why regular self-reflection is part of your strategizing. Often, these personal determinants drive your structured planning work, because you are clear about what you want to develop, apply for or move to.

But the second category – the situational determinants – is often less clear and changes more frequently. And as we've said before, that's particularly true for women. This category includes factors such as social structures, the multiple roles women play, and socio-economic issues in your part of the world, such as the types of employment contract available and support structures like childcare or bank financing which you could access. Obviously, understanding your context is important in formulating a strategy for success, so it requires regular attention. Sometimes what seems like a constraint may actually be an opportunity, and vice versa. During the Covid-19 pandemic in 2020, the requirement for many employees to work from home looked like an opportunity for increased employment flexibility. It opened up the possibility of not having to commute every day, or of living outside large cities. It suggested that it might be possible to apply for the perfect role in a location miles from home, because much of the work could be done remotely. But because families also had to cope with their children at home with neither nurseries nor schools open, the burden of both working and running the home fell on working parents. And some evidence began to emerge that this affected women disproportionately (Scott and Gratton, 2020). It wasn't always clear, though, whether these effects would persist once public institutions began to open up again. And in such turbulent times, reading the context may be hard without the insights from a test-and-learn approach. This may help you to spot which changes might be productive parts of a new plan and where you need a new map to navigate around a new obstacle.

The exercise: guidance

This exercise brings together all the insights you have generated from previous exercises, to help you build a list of *what* you want to do, what you want to take action on. Some of your insights will be completely clear to you and the action you need to take will be obvious; some will be less so and will need further exploration, and that's perfectly normal. The key thing is to be able to distinguish which is which and proceed accordingly.

Step 1

The planning worksheet at the end of this chapter gives you some space to amalgamate your key insights from the exercises, along with your purpose statement from Chapter 5. These, along with your version of your Purpose Alignment model from Chapter 6, will give you your 'agenda for change'. For example, you may already know that you want to develop some of your strengths or make some specific changes in the logistics of your life.

Step 2

You may already have implemented some small tactical changes as you have gone through the sequence of exercises, so add those to the list too. You'll be able to mark them as done – which is always enjoyable – but including them gives you a complete picture.

Step 3

Now divide your list of changes into two: those which you are clear about, and know how to do, plus a second list of those that are still too undefined to see what your next steps might be. The worksheet at the end of this chapter gives you a structure to help you, but you could use any format that works for you.

Step 4

Turn the first category – where you are clear about your next step – into some kind of plan. This might simply be a 'To Do' list or a more formal project plan. Build into your schedule some phases, pauses and prizes. Try to be clear about your priorities and your posteriorities, too, if you can. But don't add dates just yet – we'll get to that in Step 7.

Step 5

Take your second list – the things that you are not completely clear about – and try to set down in writing what it is you are attempting to explore. For example, are there opportunities for someone with your skills to work in a different sector?

Step 6

Then devise the tactical experiment which will help you answer your question. For example, could you talk to someone in your network who already works in the sector you are interested in? Could you volunteer to work on an internal project to see if you really do want to develop this as your profession? You don't need more than one such tactic for each area to start with, since this is emergent planning: your first tactical step may show you that this is not an opportunity you want to pursue any further, or it may be the start of a new direction in your thinking.

Step 7

Now take a look at your diary for the weeks and months ahead, to add some target dates to your planned actions and experiments. Do you have time and energy for a phase of action, or do you need to make some space in your schedule first? Have you booked some time off work that might give you the chance to try an experiment? Set out the phases for the next few months and decide what you want to try to get done in each phase.

EXTENSION IDEAS

- Explaining your strategy to someone else can be a very useful exercise in clarifying and testing your own thinking. Consider finding a friend who could act as your 'peer coach' when you describe what you are trying to achieve and how you plan to go about it.

- Turn your strategy implementation work into a map: literally, make a map of your *future* journey in exactly the same way that you made a map of your working life so far. Your map could take any form – as we noted in the Introduction, there are many different ways of documenting your future. For example, if you want to plot your interim steps, you might consider preparing a portolan chart. These ancient nautical charts were collections of sailing directions, showing how to get from one port to the next. In this case, they might show your route from one milestone to the next.

- If your strategy implementation approach has a large number of experiments in it, you might consider aggregating them and planning them as a market research exercise. This might allow you to structure your time on this set of activities. It might also help you to articulate exactly what it is that you are trying to learn from each experiment – and whether you have more experiments than you need at this stage.

SUMMARY

- Strategy won't help you unless you implement it: put your ideas, insights and choices into practice. Preparation is vital: thinking about both what you want to change and how you want to do it.

- This chapter covers two implementation approaches: developing a formal, step-by-step plan, and using an iterative, experimental approach in which you try things out, review, learn and redo. Sometimes the structured planning process is what you need; sometimes the experimental approach will be perfect. More often than not, it's a mix of both. This blend is described as strategic opportunism in the corporate world.

- The Strategy Triangle illustrates these two different approaches to implementation. If your next steps are internally focused on your resources and your skills in line with your purpose (as in the left-hand side of the Strategy Triangle), you'll be able to develop a structured plan for this. If, on the other hand, you are looking for external opportunities (as in the right-hand side), you have much less ability to plan for what might happen, so a more exploratory approach could be better.

- Choosing which approach to take is a function of what you want to do and how clear you are about it. If the action is obvious and you feel comfortable about it as a next step, build it into your plan. If it is not clear, take a more exploratory approach and devise some 'test-and-learn' experiments.

- Deciding what to do will come from the exercises that you have done in this book, particularly in Chapters 5 and 6. Some of the changes may be major shifts in direction, but don't forget the small strategic decisions that can also be significant: enabling factors, tiny changes in routine, or outsourcing or stopping some activities.

- You may have your own planning preferences, but the Five Ps of personal planning might be useful: focus on **priorities**, or, if that's too hard, identify the **posteriorities** that are at the bottom of your 'To Do' list; consider planning in **phases**; build in some **pauses**; and plan to give yourself small **prizes** at key milestones.

What's next?

Preparation is an important prerequisite, but this book won't have done its job until you actually take some action, no matter how small. So the final chapter focuses on the first steps as you get under way.

FIGURE 9.2 Strategy into Action worksheet

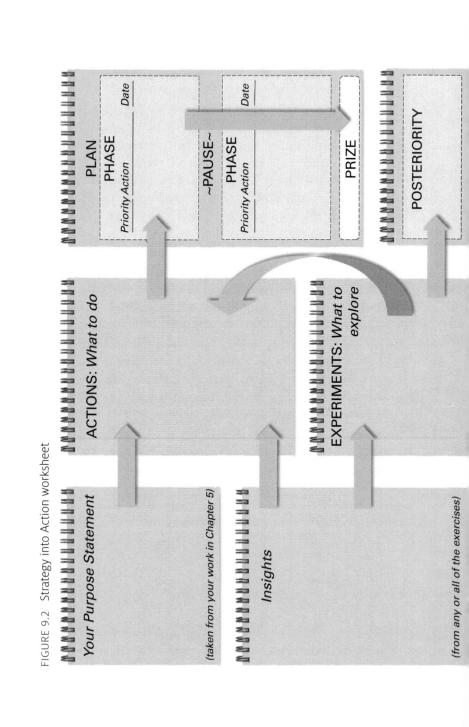

PLAN

PHASE   Date ___

Priority Action

~PAUSE~

PHASE   Date ___

Priority Action

PRIZE

POSTERIORITY

ACTIONS: *What to do*

EXPERIMENTS: *What to explore*

Your Purpose Statement

(taken from your work in Chapter 5)

Insights

(from any or all of the exercises)

CHAPTER TEN

Getting under way: tactics for taking action

What's the best way to get started on implementing your strategy?

Strategy formulation may not always be easy, but strategy implementation is *never* easy. And a good strategy doesn't automatically turn into good execution. There's a business anecdote from the 1980s about the CEO of a major computer manufacturer who sent out the headlines of his company's new strategy to all his customers and competitors in a press release. (It was sent out by fax, apparently, since it was the last century.) His senior leadership team was appalled. How could he simply give away their plans like that? When challenged, he apparently replied that it made no difference at all who saw their new strategy, because none of his competitors could or would actually do anything to implement any of it. And, of course, they didn't.

This final chapter has a different structure from the others, because it is simply intended to encourage you to take some action, no matter how small. In a book about your strategy, this chapter is about tactics. They are more important than the word implies: as Sun Tzu, the Chinese general and military strategist, apparently said: 'Strategy without tactics is the slowest route to victory; tactics without strategy is the noise before defeat.'

Tactics are really micro-strategies, small direction-setting decisions about what to do, which will move you forward in the right direction. A tactic is defined as 'a conceptual action designed to help in the achievement of a goal'. It comes from the ancient Greek word *taktike*, meaning 'the art of arrangement' – in other words, the arrangement or deployment of your resources. Tactics are actions you can take today, even when the diary looks completely full. They are decisions which we ought to make with an eye on the future, not just the present. As Alvin Toffler said: 'You've got to think about big things while you are doing small things so that all the small things go in the right direction.'

That sounds obvious, but sometimes the tactics to take you forwards seem to be taking you backwards, or at least sideways, as Chris found in the example below.

CASE STUDY Short-term tactics towards a strategic goal

Chris worked in a small marketing agency and wanted to move more into the events management side of their work. But she found herself spending too much of her time on the administration tasks that kept the organization going, including HR support for individuals and teams. She was quite good at this and her employer really valued her work in this area, but it was not what she wanted to do. She saw the problem clearly: someone needed to do the HR support work but there was literally no one else in this small, tight-knit organization. Her first objective was to make some space in her working week so that she could get involved with the staging of client events.

Her tactic was to help with the process of recruiting a new office manager, suggesting that one of the roles for this person might be to take on the HR responsibilities, if they could find someone with experience in this area. Chris had to spend time negotiating with her employer on this, since they felt that she was perfectly good at these activities. But she persisted. She also volunteered to be on the interview panel so that she could see for herself whether a candidate would be able to take on the HR role successfully. These tactics required her to spend more time in the short term on the administration functions – which was exactly what she didn't want – but she could see that she had to do this in order to make space in the medium term to achieve her goals.

Using tactics to generate strategy

There are times in your working life when you might feel that you don't have time for a strategy, maybe because you haven't had time to reflect, or the circumstances of your life are very turbulent. But taking a tactical step can help you go forwards, even if the route ahead appears fog-bound. As the road becomes clearer, other options emerge. You can learn from even the smallest tactical action, and sometimes that changes your strategic direction. For example, buying a book from the reading list of a course you think would be perfect for you might show you that you're right – or it might prove to be much duller than you thought. So is this really the course for you? And is it really a vital qualification for what you want to do? The success or failure of a particular tactic tells you something about the context and the assumptions you have made. That may be a signal that your strategic direction will lead you to success, or it could be an indication that you need to make a new map. This is how your tactics can themselves generate strategy.

If you are feeling stuck, or the careful plans that you developed in the previous chapter seem overwhelming, sometimes you just need to do something. For example, when I started writing this book, the blindingly simple truth became clear to me: if you don't put your fingers on the keyboard, the book doesn't get written. That's partly a joke, but it's also a stark truth about the importance of taking action. If I could sit at the keyboard for 10 minutes a day, something would get written, some ideas fleshed out. Just starting is sometimes more than half the battle.

Four tactics for strategy implementation

Here are four straightforward tactics which are part of almost every strategy, whether in organizations or for individuals. You might want to build these into your plan, or simply pick one and act on it. That will get you started on the next phase of your journey, using the map you have made.

Corporate scanning

One key part of the strategy formulation process in organizations is the almost constant review of what's happening in the market, what competitors are doing, and what customers want. This is not just carefully commissioned market research, but more frequent and even more superficial 'corporate scanning'. It's about staying in regular touch with what's happening or just about to happen in your context. And this is just as important for women who work as it is for companies.

Here are three simple actions you could take to help you to stay up to date and to spot opportunities which might be worth exploring:

- Read the trade press for your own sector and also adjacent sectors – even if you skim them, you'll find emerging ideas and job advertisements for new and interesting roles.

- Find someone in your network who is a recruitment consultant – they often have broad overviews of what's going on in the employment market, even if they can't help you directly right now.
- Every so often, deliberately read something about a completely different sector or organization. It might be a book or an article, chosen at random or recommended by someone whose job is completely different from yours. You might be surprised at what you learn and how useful it might be.

Networking

There is some interesting research which suggests that men and women use their networks of colleagues and contacts differently. Women tend to prefer to network for advice, while men tend to network for access to particular organizations or jobs being advertised. Neither approach is necessarily right or wrong but there are times when your network might help you to notice and access an opportunity that you would otherwise miss. So it's worth looking at what kind of network connections you have and how you interact with them. Are they largely people like you, with similar roles, working in the same industry, to whom you go for advice? This similarity allows you to build what's called 'bonding capital' (Putnam, 2000). But connecting with people who have very different jobs or work in different sectors would allow you to build 'bridging capital', increasing your exposure to different ideas and approaches. Once again, neither approach is better than the other, but, obviously, both bonding and bridging capital could be useful to you at different stages of your working life.

Networking in the virtual world presents you with various options, and you should be clear about exactly how you choose to construct and interact with your networks. Some people connect virtually only with people they know and have worked with; they could, if asked, give a reference or endorsement to each of their connections. Others choose to build wider networks, making virtual connections with a variety of people whom they have never met. You have some choices here which you might want to make consciously.

If the idea of networking makes you uncomfortable because it feels superficial or artificial, start by helping someone in your own network. By offering assistance or advice, or even letting someone know about a job advertisement, you may begin to feel differently about networking since you have something to offer yourself. Networking works best when it is a reciprocal arrangement. And it can be worth investing time in developing a wide and interesting network as a deliberate tactic.

Collaborating

At several points in this book, the extension ideas have recommended that you consider working with others as you develop your ideas and formulate your strategy. Their insights could bring a fresh perspective on issues you may be too close to or have been wrestling with for months. On the residential programmes at the Saïd Business School at the University of Oxford, participants find that working on their strategy with someone else – even someone from a completely different sector – is surprisingly useful.

Collaborating with others in the implementation phase, when you are trying to put some of your ideas into practice, can also be energizing. A trusted colleague or friend can provide support along the way. If you work with a coach, they can help you to hold yourself accountable for making some progress. But if you find yourself stuck as you start to implement your strategy, simply talking things through with someone else will often clarify your thoughts and generate a specific, useful step that you could take right now.

Personal branding

In a world of virtual connections and virtual presence, you will need to manage what the world knows about you carefully.

There are some basic things you might want to do to ensure that you are ready to seize opportunities or to increase the likelihood that they find you. There's an explicit parallel here with a company's investment in the brands they sell: you are a brand yourself, and you'll want to be sure that everything about you in the virtual or physical world says what you want it to say.

Personal branding is a marketing idea which encompasses both what the world knows about you and who knows it. It's about your narrative and your connections. You want your narrative to be consistent and your network of connections to be broad. You want to be noticed, so that opportunities find you, without looking like an arrogant self-promoter.

Is the information about you on the web consistent? Do you use social media for a range of different purposes without distinguishing between them? If your Instagram account is only for your family and mostly consists of family photos, you might want to make sure that the privacy and confidentiality settings are appropriate. If, on the other hand, you use it for work purposes too, you might want to filter what you post about your private life. What is once posted on the web never entirely goes away, even if you delete it. Many people have separate Twitter accounts for this reason – one for their professional life and one for their personal life.

As a starting point, run an audit of your online presence. If you search for your own name, what comes up? Is it you, or someone else? And if it is you, what comes up first – something appropriately professional or a personal holiday photo on Instagram? What does your LinkedIn profile say about you? Is it concise and grammatically correct? Actively managing and controlling your own narrative is vital over a long working life.

Finally, take a look at your CV, which is the most concise expression of you and your brand. Over the course of the exercises in this book, you may have gathered a set of insights about your skills and what you have done and you may want to rewrite your CV as a consequence. There is an enormous amount of advice on the web about this, and I have only one suggestion to add. Your CV needs to do two things: it should reveal the kind of person you are and be appropriate for the role you are trying to get. Achieving both objectives in one document is not always easy, but this idea certainly suggests that you will want to redraft it or tailor it for different opportunities. This is not about being inauthentic, but about demonstrating how closely your skills and experience match the criteria in the advertisement.

This idea of personal branding sounds complex, but it's simply a matter of paying attention to what you say about yourself in documents and on the web. And sometimes even a little effort in this area can pay off, as Charlotte found in the example below.

CASE STUDY One tiny tactic

Doing all the strategy exercises gave Charlotte a whole range of useful insights – almost too many. She made herself a substantial action plan, which looked rather daunting. But she really wanted to do something, just to get started, so she looked for a simple tactic to implement straight away. A quick audit of her online presence showed her that her LinkedIn profile badly needed updating. It was missing some basic information about her current role and even her current work location. 'I didn't have much time, but a few small edits and updates felt like progress,' she commented. 'And it had some effect. Oddly, within a week of updating my profile, I had a call from a recruitment consultant about a job in my location. To be honest, I was a bit suspicious since it looked as if it was just my location which had made my name come up on the consultant's search, but I thought I would go and talk to them – and it turned out to be really quite interesting. I'd never thought about a job with that particular organization before!'

Even the smallest tactic can produce a result, opening up a new opportunity. So if you can, find some time to add the four tactics in this chapter to your plans, because at some point on the journey they could bring some real benefit.

Getting under way

This book has been written as a vade mecum, to go with you on the journey through your working life, to help you to find success at every stage. If you've gone through the strategizing process and done some of the exercises in this book, you deserve congratulations. You will now be much clearer about what you want from your working life, where you want to be and how to get there. You'll have made your own map. You will also be a more expert map-maker, so that when things change around you, as they will, you can adapt your map accordingly. So now it's time to get under way.

SUMMARY

- Strategy implementation is always demanding, harder even than formulating strategy, but this book won't have served its purpose until you are able to take some actions in line with your new strategy.

- Even a tactical step will help you to get under way. Tactics are an integral part of strategy: they are micro-strategies, small direction-setting decisions about what to do, which will move you forward in the right direction. The word 'tactic' is defined as a conceptual action designed to help in the achievement of a goal.

- Tactics are also sources of feedback about how your strategy is working in the real world. The lessons you learn may cause you to change direction or to make a whole new map of where you want to get to and how.

- There are four particular tactics which are worth considering because they are important, doable actions which will help you to learn about what works and what doesn't. They are:

- corporate scanning;

- networking;

- collaborating;

- personal branding.

• If you do nothing else, put one of these tactics into action and you will be under way.

References

Preface: why this book is for you

Ruderman, M A et al (2002) Benefits of multiple roles for managerial women, *Academy of Management Journal*, **45** (2) pp. 369–86

Introduction

Buckingham, M (2008) *The One Thing You Need to Know about Great Managing, Great Leading and Sustained Individual Success*, Simon and Schuster, New York, p. 219

Super, D E (1980) A life-span, life-space approach to career development, *Journal of Vocational Behaviour*, **16**, pp. 282–98

Wiseman, R (2009) *59 Seconds: Think a little, change a lot*, Macmillan, London

Chapter 1

Alexander, M, Strategy Triangle model adapted from teaching material used at the Saïd Business School, University of Oxford

Alexander, M and Campbell, A (1997) What's wrong with strategy, *Harvard Business Review*, November–December

Norman, D (1993) *Things that Make Us Smart: Defending human attributes in the age of the machine*, Perseus Books, New York

Chapter 2

Chisholm, K, Swart, T and Brown, P (2015) *Neuroscience for Leadership*, Palgrave Macmillan, Basingstoke, p. 117

Ruddle, K (1999) Understanding journeys of transformation: exploring new paradigms in strategic change and enterprise transformation, D. Phil. thesis, University of Oxford. Available from: https://ora.ox.ac.uk/objects/uuid:ffb6a092-8476-4a07-899b-be41d4037caa (archived at https://perma.cc/P5J5-MYAN)

Chapter 3

Athanasopoulou, A, Moss-Cowan, A, Smets, M and Morris, T (2017) Claiming the corner office: female CEO careers and implications for leadership development, *Human Resource Management*, 57 (2), pp. 617–39

Chapter 4

Garcia, H and Miralles, F (2017) *Ikigai: The Japanese secret to a long and happy life*, translated by H Clearly, Hutchinson, London

Hasegawa, A (2019) *Ikigai According to Professor Akihiro Hasegawa*, episode 1, 20 November [podcast] www.ikigaitribe.com (archived at https://perma.cc/78F9-CAFS)

Tamashiro, T (2019) *How to Ikigai: Lessons for finding happiness and living your life's purpose*, Mango Publishing Group, Coral Gables, USA

Chapter 5

Avon (2020) Our company story [online] www.avonworldwide.com (archived at https://perma.cc/M64Y-XG5P) and www.avon.uk.com (archived at https://perma.cc/WKQ3-ESYY)

Financial Reporting Council (2020) *Annual Review of the UK Corporate Governance Code January 2020*, Financial Reporting Council, London

Jacobs, R (2017) *The 7 Questions to Find Your Purpose*, Watkins, London

Matthews, A (1997) *Follow Your Heart: Finding purpose in your life and work*, Seashell Publishers, Trinity Beach, Australia

Mead, G (2014) *Telling the Story: The heart and soul of successful leadership*, Wiley and Sons, London

Sinek, S (2009) *Start with Why*, Portfolio Penguin, New York

Sinek, S, Mead, D and Docker, P (2017) *Find Your Why: A practical guide for discovering purpose for you and your team*, Penguin, London

Chapter 6

Belmond (2019) Careers Open Day: Belmond Le Manoir aux Quat'Saisons, Monday 2 September 2019 [online] www.caterer.com/job/careers-open-day-belmond-le-manoir-aux-quat-saisons/belmond-le-manthe goodoir-aux-quat-saisons-job87511616

Belmond (2020) Excellence in Oxfordshire [online] www.belmond.com/ideas/articles/belmond-le-manoir-aux-quat-saisons (archived at https://perma.cc/6634-UDRE)

Belmond Le Manoir (2020) *About us* [online] www.belmond.com/hotels/europe/uk/oxfordshire/belmond-le-manoir-aux-quat-saisons/about (archived at https://perma.cc/6P38-GLV8)

McDonalds (2020) Careers [online] https://people.mcdonalds.co.uk/ (archived at https://perma.cc/E2P3-HX9L)

Manzoori-Stamford, J (2012) Le Manoir aux Quatre Saisons wins four trophies at the springboard awards, *The Caterer*, 19 October [online] www.thecaterer.com/news/foodservice/le-manoir-aux-quatsaisons-wins-four-trophies-at-the-springboard-awards (archived at https://perma.cc/4FTC-SRH7)

Neate, R (2015) McDonald's: a brief history in 15 facts [online] www.theguardian.com/business/2015/may/02/mcdonalds-a-brief-history-in-15-facts (archived at https://perma.cc/5AUJ-TS37)

Smith, C (2020) 50 McDonalds statistics and facts [online] https://expandedramblings.com/index.php/mcdonalds-statistics/ (archived at https://perma.cc/5YZ8-5AP5)

The Drum (2013) Recruitment Business Awards 2013 [online] www.
recruitmentbusinessawards.com/recruitment-business-awards/
recruitment-business-awards-2013#49629 (archived at https://perma.cc/
VX99-BGWT)

Trevor, J (2019) *Align: A leadership blueprint for aligning enterprise
purpose, strategy and organisation*, Bloomsbury Business, London

Chapter 7

Pendleton, D and Furnham, A (2012) *Leadership: All you need to know*,
Palgrave Macmillan, London

Chapter 8

Ansoff, I (1957) Strategies for diversification, *Harvard Business Review*,
35 (5), pp. 113–24

Monty Python's Flying Circus (1969) *Vocational Guidance Counsellor*,
episode 10

Chapter 9

Drucker, P F (2002) *The Effective Executive*, Harper Business Essentials,
New York

Franklin, B (1758) The way to wealth, American Literature Research and
Analysis Website, Florida Gulf Coast University [online]

Golzen, G and Garner, A (1990) *Smart Moves: Successful strategies and
tactics for career management*, Blackwell, Oxford

Isenberg, D (1987) The tactics of strategic opportunism, *Harvard Business
Review*, www.hbr.org (archived at https://perma.cc/9Q2E-4BQ2)

Mann, S (2004) Learning for a lifetime, *Professional Manager*, 13 (2),
pp. 28–29

Scott, A and Gratton, L (2020) New ways of living, *The Sunday Times*, 24
May, www.times.com (archived at https://perma.cc/EQN3-LPVA)

Super, D E (1980) A life-span, life-space approach to career development, *Journal of Vocational Behaviour*, **16**, pp. 282–98

von Moltke, H, cited in *Oxford Essential Quotations* (2016) [online] www.oxfordreference.com/view/10.1093/acref/9780191826719.001. 0001/q-oro-ed4-00007547 (archived at https://perma.cc/9TRD-QF7T)

Williamson, P J (1999) Strategy as options for the future, *MIT Sloan Management Review*, www.sloanreview.mit.edu (archived at https://perma.cc/9DQ4-WVAF)

Chapter 10

Jackson, E (2014) Sun Tzu's 31 best pieces of leadership advice, *Forbes*, 23 May [online] www.forbes.com/sites/ericjackson/2014/05/23/ sun-tzus-33-best-pieces-of-leadership-advice/#1e766e2c5e5e (archived at https://perma.cc/97VR-V9MZ)

Putnam, R D (2000) *Bowling Alone: The collapse and revival of American community*, Simon and Schuster, New York

Toffler, A, cited in LeadershipQuote [online] www.leadershipquote.org/ youve-got-to-think-about-the-big-things/ (archived at https://perma. cc/9K38-XDZX)

Further reading

Alboher, M (2012) *The Encore Career Handbook: How to make a living and a difference in the second half of life*, Workman Publishing, New York

Boldt, L (1999) *Zen and the Art of Making a Living: A practical guide to creative career design*, Penguin Books, New York

Burnett, B and Evans, D (2016) *Designing Your Life*, Knopf, New York

Carson, N (2012) *The Finch Effect: The five strategies to adapt and thrive in your working life*, Jossey-Bass, San Francisco

Clark, T, Osterwalder, A and Pigneur, Y (2012) *Business Model You: A one page method for reinventing your career*, Wiley and Sons, London

Clayton, C and Allworth, J (2012) *How Will You Measure Your Life?* HarperCollins, London

Dent, F, Holton, V and Rabbetts, J (2011) *Understanding Women's Careers*, Ashridge, Berkhamsted

Drucker, P (2010) Managing yourself, in *On Managing Yourself*, Harvard Business Review Press, Boston

Erickson, T J (2008) *Retire Retirement: Career strategies for the boomer generation*, Harvard Business Press, Boston

Gannon, M (2018) *The Multi-hyphen Method*, Hodder and Stoughton, London

Golzen, G and Garner, A (1992) *Smart Moves: Successful strategies and tactics for career management*, Penguin Books, London

Gratton, L and Scott, A (2017) *The 100-year Life: Living and working in and age of longevity*, Bloomsbury, London

Ibarra, H (2004) *Working Identity: Unconventional strategies for reinventing your career*, Harvard Business Review Press, Boston

Krznaric, R (2012) *How to Find Fulfilling Work*, Macmillan, London

McDaniels, C (1989) *The Changing Workplace: Career counselling strategies for the 1990s and beyond*, Jossey-Bass, San Francisco

Pfeffer, J and Sutton, R I (1999) *The Knowing–Doing Gap: How smart companies turn knowledge into action*, Harvard Business School Press, Boston

Rubin, G (2015) *Better Than Before: What I learned about making and breaking habits*, Hachette, London

Scheele, A (1994) *Career Strategies for the Working Woman*, Simon and Schuster, New York

Sheehy, G (1996) *New Passages: Mapping your life across time*, HarperCollins, London

Slaughter, A M (2012) Why women still can't have it all, *The Atlantic*, July/August, www.theatlantic.com/magazine/archive/2012/07/why-women-still-cant-have-it-all/309020 (archived at https://perma.cc/C62U-5Q7J)

Index